For Love of the British Isles: Anglophile Diaries through the Decades

Nan Pendergrast

Photographs by Britt Pendergrast

Nature's Face Publications

2015

Copyright ©2015 by Nan Schwab Pendergrast

ISBN: 978-0-9829004-6-8

All rights reserved. No part of this document may be reproduced or transmitted in any form or by any means, electronic, mechanical, photocopying, recording, or otherwise, without prior written permission from the copyright holder.

Printed in the United States of America.

Cover design: John Pendergrast III

Send comments or corrections to John Pendergrast, pendergrast.john@yahoo.ca

Table of Contents

Foreword — page 1

Prelude: Ascot, England, 1938 — page 3

Ireland and England, 1961 — page 9

England – May-June, 1985 — page 81

England – Spring, 1999 — page 133

Afterword — page 161

Foreword

This book primarily consists of the journals I wrote during and after three trips I took with my husband Britt to the British Isles in 1961, 1985 and 1999, along with recollections of my first trip to England with my parents as an eighteen-year-old in 1938.

Let me explain how this book came to be. One of my daughters-in-law, knowing my enduring love for the British Isles, gave me a book by an American woman who had traveled there. I was grateful, but as I read the book, I became annoyed at how self-centered her account was -- readers learned more about her tastes and prejudices than about the places she went.

I thought of my own journals and hoped they did not sound quite so egoistic. I was relieved when I unearthed them from my files to find that they were actually quite interesting and informative. I mentioned this to my son Mark, who had helped edit and publish my previous book, *Neighborhood Naturalist*, and he asked to look at them, too. He did some preliminary edits, along with his friend Martin Hirschfeld, and then asked my oldest son, John, to take over the project for fact-checking and further editing. Britt, my husband of 75 years, took photos during our trips that are included here as illustrations. The result is the book you are holding in your hands.

Britt and I no longer travel much. It has been – can it be? – almost nine decades since I was a little girl gazing longingly across the Atlantic from the shores of a Georgia barrier island. I dreamed of floating across to the magic land of Mother Goose and Christopher Robin. I thought it was Ireland I would reach, and it was a surprise to find later that, had my journey been directly to the east, as I'd imagined, I'd have landed in North Africa. My actual trips by ocean liner and then by airplane all veered northeast to reach those Emerald Isles. The reality I discovered on arrival surpassed all my childish imaginings.

To say that I love the British Isles is like saying I love my husband. It is true, but the bare statement leaves out all that matters – the learning, the growing, the developing and deepening of the relationship. My love affair with Ireland, England, Scotland, and Wales didn't happen all at once. The journals that follow record the adventure, charm, beauty, and mystery of this ancient land and my discovery of it. I hope you enjoy reliving the trips as much as I have.

--Nan Pendergrast

Prelude: Ascot, England, 1938

It has always seemed to me very evident that, as my own life is my most valuable possession, so too must be the life of any creature to him. When I was a child, if a playmate stepped on a bug, I cringed. As I grew old enough to read, it seemed even clearer that, as our friend Jeannette Rankin explained when she cast the lone vote in Congress against entry into World War II, "No international problem has ever been solved by the killing of young men." Traveling in England in 1938, I learned at first hand why wars are fought.

We were visiting in Ascot, at the country home of the Ostrers. My parents had met Karen Petersen, now Mrs. O., when she and her parents had spent their holidays in Wisconsin, where we went every summer. We knew that to the horror of her physician father she had gone to New York and become a dancer on the stage, and later we heard that she had gone to England with a show and had met and married an Englishman. Until my father phoned her from London and she insisted that we come down for the weekend, however, we had no idea how spectacularly *well* she had married.

Mark Ostrer at the time of our stay was the president of the largest film company in the country, one of six brothers who owned banks, newspapers, and various other enterprises. There were eighteen guests for the weekend, ranging from a third-rate vaudevillian, whom Karen had known during her days on the stage, who was honeymooning with his third wife, to a Scots doctor who had been invited at the last moment to make us feel at home, because he had once played golf with our fellow townsman Bobby Jones. His name was Archie Tanbourne – besides playing golf he was physician to the royal family.

The two Great Danes owned by the Ostrers made me feel at home, since I had Danes as pets, but the splendor of the surroundings was unlike any place I had ever stayed – the house was a huge rambling structure of no particular architectural style, with so vast a number of rooms that our sleeping place was only to be found by a card on the door. Karen did not know how many servants there were, but when Mark Ostrer glanced over my shoulder to read the letter I was writing to Britt, he corrected the "butlers behind every chair" I had reported, saying, "There is never more than one butler. The rest are footmen." There was a Hollywood air about the place, with its tennis courts, large swimming pool, stables and rings, and the first privately owned squash court I had ever seen. And I was not the only one to be impressed. When the Hurst-Brown brothers who lived next door came to swim and invited me home to tea, their mother made it clear that no one else lived like the Osters.

Among the other guests was a fat, usually hung–over fellow who sat swathed in a large towel by the pool each morning. He was, I learned to my surprise, , head of the Royal Air Force. I was not surprised when, a few years later, he lost North Africa to the Germans.

There was also an elderly, white-mustachioed man with an accent, who asked me every morning what I thought of the stock market's performance the day before. And then there was Stephen Raphael, a pudgy fellow ten years my senior, who had become, one of the footmen told me, the wealthiest bachelor in England since the Duke of Norfolk had taken a bride three weeks earlier. Finally, there was a German named Felix Goetz. Mark Ostrer, Felix Goetz, Stephen Raphael and Air Vice-Marshal Welch closeted themselves in the library for hours every day, seldom emerging into the glorious summer days.

Ostrer sons with a junior Rolls (photo by Robert Schwab)

As we drove back to London, I remarked on this strange practice to my father, who explained to me that, in this summer of '38, war was sure to come. The three men were busy arranging that, when it did come, no one on either side would bomb the oil field they owned jointly in Ploesti, Romania. War came on schedule the following year, and Stephen came to New York City to sit out the unpleasantness in the bistros, while Felix Goetz returned to his position in Berlin as chief financial advisor to Hitler.

I watched during the mounting carnage of the war years, and no one touched Ploesti until August 1, 1943, when the Americans, who had evidently not been told about the cozy arrangement, finally bombed it.

Only Mrs. Ostrer contributed to the war effort, and she may have been moved as much by boredom and nostalgia for her brief stage career as by patriotism. She persuaded her husband to finance a revival of her show and took it touring for the troops throughout the British Isles. I hope they enjoyed it during its brief run – Mrs. Ostrer caught pneumonia in Brighton and died.

When I went back to England about twenty years after the war, Mr. Ostrer had remarried. His nephew, Christopher, who was eighteen and had emulated his uncle by marrying a showgirl in '38, was written up in the London Times in 1961 – he was being sued by another showgirl for refusing to support their baby.

All of this goes a bit towards explaining my husband Britt's and my skepticism at the chauvinistic excesses of all the participants in the war, and Britt's refusal to kill for the cause. Economic advantage, it seemed to us, played a disproportionate part in the proceedings, for all that our papers trumpeted truthfully the ghastliness of the Nazis. From the beginning, in the early thirties when Jewish refugees brought word of increasing repression, we worked for an economic boycott while American manufacturers continued to supply scrap iron for the arms buildup of both Germany and Japan.

One other incident stands out from my first visit to England as a teenager in 1938. I loved the A. A. Milne poem that went:

> They're changing guard at Buckingham Palace –
> Christopher Robin went down with Alice.
> Alice is marrying one of the guard.
> "A soldier's life is terribly hard," says Alice.

Nan with guard at Buckingham Palace (photo by Robert Schwab)

—Naturally, when I got to London, I had to go to Buckingham Palace, too. As my father and I watched the guards marching impassively back and forth, Daddy bet me a quarter that I couldn't make one of them smile. So I marched alongside one and told him of the wager. He beckoned me to follow him, and we turned a corner to get out of public sight. He suggested we exchange addresses and obligingly smiled as my father took a picture of us. I collected my bet and inaugurated a correspondence once I was back in Atlanta. His name was Arthur Wilson. He was twenty-one years old and longed to come to America. Later he wrote that he'd had the honor and unease of being selected one of four Coldstream Guards to stand with his back to the coffin containing the corpse of a Scandinavian queen, one of Queen Victoria's nine grandchildren, through a long, scary night.

    Then he wrote that he was being shipped to Palestine. There he escaped being hit by a sniper. After that, he wrote, "You must hate me. I've killed a man." I wrote that I understood and hoped we'd meet some day in Georgia. Then there was only silence.

Ireland and Brilliant Green England, 1961

Heavy, mundane, seemingly as earthbound but not nearly so speedy as the cars whizzing past on the highway that paralleled the landing strip, our plane lumbered along, twelfth in line for takeoff. I was with my husband Britt, and behind us lay twenty years of dreaming and numberless hours of reading. I had fantasized about the lake country of Wordsworth and Walpole, the Cornwall of Daphne du Maurier, the eglantine and columbine of Shakespeare's magic forests and the highlands of his Macbeth, the lochs of Scott and Burns, the Ireland extolled by Yeats, lacerated by Joyce and lyricized by at least a dozen homesick Irish-Americans. Now, with only a few hours of flying between me and the Isles, I wondered uneasily if they might all prove as mythical as Angela Thirkell's delightful Barsetshire, as unreal, or vanished forever, as the white-columned magnolia-drenched South which all readers know well, a land with which we natives are not even faintly familiar.

As our plane limped back to the hangar to have a faulty spark plug replaced, a very small shove would have sent me limping homeward too, untraveled but with illusions intact. I'm grateful that nobody pushed, and that the next morning Ireland finally rose out of the mist beneath our wings. Its green fields extended to the very shores of the ocean, and the gray stone walls which patterned the pastures seemed merely to accentuate the glow of that unbelievably brilliant hue. The cottages were primrose-yellow.

My misgivings about modernity returned when we landed at Shannon Airport, a bright, modern, bustling international building. The young man who had our rented car waiting gave us driving instructions in a business-like voice, with only a bare hint of brogue. I wondered sadly what had become of Irish inefficiency.

First Glimpse of Ireland

      Within a matter of moments, however, we had left the twentieth century behind and were driving along a narrow road, bordered by grey stone walls, over which greenery spilled from the fields they sought to enclose. We neither met, nor overtook, any other automobiles. In fact, the road seemed completely deserted until we rounded a curve and found a herd of sheep meandering down the middle of the road. They were tended by a lackadaisical shepherd and a dog that seemed more intent upon chasing a crow that flew suddenly up from the roadside than leading his stupid but sweet charges out of harm's way.

We had resumed our rushed American pace when, around another curve, we encountered another surprise – a gigantic building of heavy stone. It was our first castle, and we were in too tearing a hurry to do more than glimpse a single, self-effacing sign, which whispered that the grounds and the castle were open to the public. On we went to Limerick, nine miles distant, where rooms awaited us at the Arthur Guesthouse, a Victorian mansion now converted to a hotel.

The establishment was run by two maiden ladies, sisters who shared a love of their country and a certain tartness of manner and speech. Through them I learned that I had made a tactical error. In writing ahead for the car and this first night's accommodations, I had mentioned that our trip was a return to the land of my husband's forebears (Prendergast is the original Irish spelling.)

Ireland, our hostesses now informed us, welcomed all tourists, but not so much the Irish who had done well in the States and who could be suspected of returning to the mother country to lord it over the poverty-stricken relations who had stayed home. To a lesser degree, this distaste extended to the descendants of such emigrants. Afterwards we made no mention of whence Britt's great-great-grandparents had sprung.

After setting down our suitcases, we took ourselves off to see the town of Limerick, our first stop being King John's Castle. Our guide there, a cheerfully irascible old fellow, expressed, with equal gusto, his distaste for the English, the recent Hungarian refugees, and the sun, which had had the temerity to shine for two weeks in a row, raising the temperature to a sweltering and unprecedented eighty degrees. The Irish greatly prefer what is called a "soft" day – a gentle mist.

The original thick stone walls of the castle enclosed a barracks built by the English during some part of their seven hundred year occupation of Ireland. Now these barracks served as living quarters for six families, who had fifty-six children in all. The grim walls of the castle were abloom with dandelions and brilliant yellow wallflowers, and below them the pony carts clattered over the bridge across the river, while fishermen waded in the clear water. It was a peaceful scene, but such tranquility had so newly come that the Irish seemed, at times, to be a bit lost without an enemy. Our guide pointed downriver where, during the potato famine of 1845, grain boats sent by the Greeks to feed the starving Irish had been sunk by the English.

From the castle tower could be seen the walls of the old town of Limerick, founded by the Danes in the ninth century. It was now a thriving city of fifty thousand inhabitants, which boasted much new building and no slums.

The weather was more to our guide's liking than ours, being moist and chilly, and it led to a terrible gastronomical error. We thought, when ordering lunch, that Brown Windsor Soup would be a good beginning, figuring that anything warm would be welcome. This glop was composed, we decided, of all the drippings off the stove plus enough dishwater to ensure the proper consistency.

According to the latest studies of the UN, Ireland at that time was the best fed country in the world, and we found the food plentiful and reasonably priced. However, it was more adequate than inspiring, except for a mouthwatering experience at Bailey's Restaurant in Dublin, where the prawn cocktails made every subsequent seafood adventure seem anti-climactic, and where the steak was kissed effectively by herbs.

Be that as it may, Ireland's secure place in our memories was attained through her people and her scenery, and we got a sampling of both our first afternoon there. We retraced our steps to Bunratty Castle, which we had sped past earlier, and at first thought the small sign announcing that it was open to the public was in error. There was no visible entry, no crowds, and no cars parked anywhere. We prowled around to the back, where a lone bicycle propped near an unmarked and insignificant entry gave us a clue that the place might indeed be tenanted. We entered the vast stone structure, and shivering with awe and chill, crept along the lengthy corridors until we found ourselves in a vast hall. There, tucked into one corner, was a desk covered with brochures about Ireland, and behind the desk sat a young man deep in a book. He glanced up, nodded, smiled, and went back to his book. When we asked if there were an admission charge, he confessed shamefacedly that there was, but he appeared to be comforted by the fact that we had no Irish currency as yet, and he professed inability to change our American money. We wandered the length, breadth and height of the place, which were considerable, as his guests.

The castle was originally built in 1210, but it is to

the period of its greatest splendor – mid-fifteenth century – that the government has restored it. We saw the furniture, the cooking utensils, the splendor of its great halls, the discomfort of its bedchambers, and the horror of its dungeons, and thought that we did not envy the infant William Penn, who, with his family, was once besieged there.

    Back at Arthur House, our scholarly and somewhat acid hostess cut through our ravings about Bunratty Castle with the chill remark that many of the furnishings were not mid-fifteenth century at all, but late-fifteenth, and in a few reprehensible cases, actually sixteenth century. Our ignorance had led us to a thorough enjoyment of everything, including a magnificently impressive specimen of *Megaceros Hibernicus* glaring from the wall of the great dining hall. Even we realized at the time that the Irish elk antedated the castle, since it had been extinct for some two thousand years. Due to a natural embalming fluid present in the bogs of Ireland, specimens of this tremendous animal, complete with hide and hair, have been exhumed. Seeing one, it is difficult to believe that its last living cousin walked the earth before Christ was born.

    A drive down to Killiloe, an Irish village whose visual beauty surpassed even the loveliness of its name, finished off our afternoon. We were pretty drowsy, having slept only in snatches on the trip over the Atlantic the night before, and I had trouble convincing my brain that the extraordinary brilliance of the grassy pasture and the glory of the deep pink apple blossoms were not part of an unrealistic but picturesque dream. My life has seldom held more frustrating moments than those during the drive through the Irish countryside, when I frantically forced my heavy eyelids to prop open only to have them droop immediately. I was convinced that I was missing my only chance to savor such beauty, and it was a delightful surprise to find later that almost all of Ireland is equally enchanting.

A look at a map proves that Ireland lies north of Newfoundland, but the temperature is far more clement and consistent, thanks to the Gulf Stream. Those who like their days soft get their wish two days out of three, and though the Irish tend to ignore all precipitation, which they refer to as "a little mist," it amounts to a moist 55 inches per year and accounts for verdant meadows wherever the drainage is sufficient, and the bogs wherever it is not.

It seems ironic that this land, surely among the most beautiful in the world, cannot support all its people. The Irish are a prolific race, and those who tarry produce many offspring and seem to adore them. After spending a day or two in Ireland, I came to look upon the mother whose pram contained only one small passenger as a piker, for by far the majority of these magnificent vehicles (prams are used for transporting preschool children, but also for hauling groceries and even coal) had one supine infant and a slightly older brother or sister riding in a small seat attached to the rear of the carriage. Usually several other children walked alongside. Yet the population of the island at the time of our trip – four million – was only half what it had been a century ago.

Behind these figures lurked the tragedy of the Emerald Isle, for at least half of these cherished children were marked for export. They would emigrate to America or England or Australia, where they would prove willing, tireless workers with one overriding goal – to earn enough to go home again.

Since independence was finally attained in 1949, however, progress has been underway, and perhaps there will be a living for all in the not-too-distant future. The student from Cork University who shared a ride with us through Killarney was the son of a contractor, and he reported that building was brisk. There was also considerable German and Japanese capital now being invested. We saw a tremendous plant for the manufacture of cranes constructed, somewhat incongruously, it seemed to me, on the shores of Lake Killarney. There were two reasons for locating it here – the hope of entrance in the European Common Market, and the vast potential labor market – in addition to the Irish at home, there were twelve million abroad eager to return.

The right-hand drive situation, which we had feared, was not too serious in Ireland, partly because we seemed most of the time to be the only automobile on the road. That did not mean we were alone. Automobiles were greatly outnumbered by cyclists, pony or donkey carts, cows, sheep, and pedestrians. Several of the latter accepted our offer to share our Anglia Ford, and in return shared with us much of the lore of their land. Mr. Corrigan, one of Ireland's many aging bachelors, rode with us to Tralee and insisted on introducing us to his neighbor, Joe Prendergast. Joe was a fine, strapping broth of a lad who played fine football, boxed well, owned three hundred acres and much stock, and was engaged to a girl recently named the Rose of Boston. Mr. Corrigan was so proud of this last bit of information that we did not dare ask who in the name of heaven the Rose of Boston was, but later someone in Dublin explained that each year Boston sent its loveliest daughter of Irish descent on a trip to Tralee.

    Our drive through southern Ireland was a succession of glorious views. Personally I prefer quiet pastoral scenes, while Britt tends toward the spectacular, but we were both indulged. Our only complaint was the utter lack of commercialism. On almost every slope stood the ruins of a gaunt gray castle, with the omnipresent crows flying through roofless towers but with absolutely no markers of any sort to inform the curious and interested traveler who lived there and when. And it was only because Ted, our university student passenger, told us its whereabouts that we found Tore Falls, a spot of incredible beauty overlooking the lakes of Killarney. On the shores of the celebrated blue waters were green pastures filled with sheep, and immediately surrounding us at the top of the falls were massive rhododendrons just bursting into brilliant bloom (the climate, which makes a hot water bottle in bed a welcome comfort even in May, is perfect for the flowers; when we left nearly four weeks later, the rhododendron was unchanged – still just bursting into bloom!)

    We spent the night in the resort village of Glengarriff, where the lively lass who served our supper had the thickest brogue we'd yet encountered. She, in her turn, found us completely incomprehensible, and at length resorted to holding the menu out for us to point to the desired items. She did manage to tell us that there would be a dance that evening, and we climbed into our bed expecting to be lulled to sleep by jigs or lullabies. Alas, what we got, at full volume, was American rock and roll, a blow intensified by the fact that, when the music finally ceased, we were treated to a further serenade by a balky motor bike, which refused to start just beneath our window.

Between Glengarriff and Bantry came a wild stretch of country – barren gray hills ending in the turbulent gray waters of Bantry Bay. Except for the persistent golden gorse, there was little sign of the lush vegetation we had seen everywhere else on the Emerald Isle. It was easy to believe that banshees wailed in the winds which whipped these stark hills rising against a misty sky. Paradoxically, the most substantial homes we had yet observed lined the roads.

Mellowness returned soon; the road to Cork threads rolling green hills and a prosperous countryside. In the city itself, we saw a museum which traced the history of the city from the Bronze Age people, of whose life 1300 years before Christ many relics were displayed, to the marble bust of Cork's most recent martyr, the last mayor of this bustling borough who served under British rule. Gaunt, eagle-nosed and proud, he died in prison in 1920 after a hunger strike in protest against the British oppression.

As we left the city, driving northward toward Dublin, we picked up Vincent Leahy, an eighteen-year-old apprentice accountant who proved to be a remarkably well-informed young man. True, he had a few cherished misapprehensions about the United

States – that the average American family had at least ten children and that all Americans were alcoholics, and he seemed almost disappointed when we did not nestle neatly into either category, but so far as his own beloved land was concerned, he was a veritable treasury of information. Not only was he able to inform us of the political and economic life of Ireland, but he also proved invaluable during one of the many times when the Irish lack of commercialism proved irritating.

    We were anxious to see the Rock of Cashel, and we detoured a bit on our way to Dublin in order to do so. However, without Vincent to guide us, we would never have found this impressive and historic spot. It was not only unmarked, it was downright hidden. It was not surprising that we were utterly alone, except for the inevitable crows and a few sheep, as we explored the ruins of a cathedral built in the eleventh century. The Irish explain the unexpected presence of the huge rock on which the cathedral is constructed with a typical bit of barbed Celtic whimsy. It seems that the devil left his home in England for a holiday, and while flying over Ireland saw a tasty-looking mountain. He flew down for a bite, and being a greedy English devil (there is no other kind) he attempted to gulp more than he could swallow, and was forced to spit out a chunk. This tale also explains an irregularly shaped mountain in the vicinity.

    Cromwell's men attacked Cashel in their rapacious march through Ireland, and having killed all the men in the village at the foot of the hill, advanced on the cathedral where the women and children had taken refuge. Their sanctuary was dishonored, and five thousand were massacred. It is said that the Protector, when one of his soldiers demurred at the slaughter of children, justified his unspeakable brutality by pointing out that "Nits grow up to make lice.

We were amused when Vincent told us why the Irish appeared to be two separate races. There are the dark-haired, fair-skinned Irish, with their sooty-lashed blue eyes, and there are the strawberry-blond, freckled, and somewhat stupid-looking lot. Vincent told us that this latter group were, of course, descendants of the English!

Next we paused at Kildare, where the Irish government owned the National Stud (pronounced like the past tense of the verb stand) Farm, which was formerly the property of the Lord Lieutenant (pronounced *leftenant*) of Ireland. There was a lovely, if somewhat incongruous, Japanese garden there. It was authentic, having been constructed with much time, effort, and expense by four Japanese gardeners imported especially for the task.

The gardens, all done in the miniature manner so necessary in crowded Japan, seemed a bit silly when, standing atop one of the tiny mountains representing triumph, one looked beyond the borders of the estate itself to see the vast lushness of Ireland!

On to Dublin, city of the Abbey Theatre, the University with its famed Book of Kels, parks and palaces, and yet, withal, a small town in its friendliness and informality. At rush hours, the streets seemed to writhe with cyclists, many of them gripping bouquets of brilliant flowers. At noon, St. Stephen's Green on a sunny day was crowded with nature-worshippers, some lying relaxed on the lawns, others combining their lunch hour with the favorite Irish pastime –

heated debate.

The Irish have, along with their often ironic charm and whimsy, an almost shocking ability see themselves as they really are. Thus the play which we saw at the Abbey Theatre dealt with the trials of transplanted Irishmen working in Birmingham. The hero, a handsome lad fresh from the ould sod with an endearing way to match his brogue, developed, during the course of the play, into a rotten lout, and it was made clear by the author, a thin, bespectacled youngster who came onstage at the end of the performance to take a bow, that this degeneration was not merely the result of unfit surroundings. No, our lad was black from the start, and was presented as typical of a group who used their years of oppression as an excuse for utter selfishness and greed.

An Irish story, reputedly occurring as two men departed the theatre after seeing a performance by an aging thespian, has one say to the other sadly, "You know, he's not the man he used to be — but then he never was..." And the witty, scholarly Mr. Darcy, who showed us about the chapel at the Palace, told us of the magnificent cathedral donated to the city of Cork by a hard-fisted industrialist, one O'Dwyer. The cathedral, dedicated during the old age of its giver, was officially named The Cathedral of Christ the King, but it was always referred to as "O'Dwyer's Fire Escape"...

It was Mr. Darcy, too, who pointed out that the carved angel hovering above the pew marked by Cromwell's name had no wings and a horrified look. The chapel was once for the use of the English governors, and its pews were marked with the names of those who fell into disfavor at home and were banished to Ireland and its unwilling subjects. Cornwallis was there, fresh from his defeat in the overseas colonies, and Cromwell early in his troublemaking days. It seemed strange that there were exactly enough pews to house the governors of Ireland, and our informant remarked that, had the Irish known this all along, the chapel would have been built on a smaller scale.

    The countryside near Dublin was entrancing. Killiney was compared by Shaw most favorably to the Bay of Naples, and our discovery of it was about as complicated as Balboa's search for the Pacific. Road signs are printed in large Gaelic letters and infinitesimal English ones, and the pronunciation of the former was so improbable as to make the asking of directions impossible. For instance, we sought the village of Dun Laoghaire, which Britt pronounced phonetically, while I struggled and came up proudly with the "gh" sound I'd heard throatily voiced throughout our trip. When both efforts met with complete incomprehension, we were reduced to pointing to the name on our map, and our informant responded, "O, ye'll be meanin' Dunleary!" It was coat-cold that day, but there were intrepid souls swimming in the bay. It seemed strange to me to stand looking out to sea and thinking, "On the other side of that water lies home."

    This entire record is a painfully honest account of my reactions, so, although Britt has practically pointed out that, due to the geographical peculiarities of Ireland, it was actually England on the far side of that water, I was thinking the above-mentioned thought just the same. So often had I stood, looking yearningly out from the shore at Sea Island, Georgia, realizing that somewhere, beyond that uninterrupted horizon, lay Ireland. The reality had not diminished the dream, and we left for England with the determination to return some day.

It is, of course, just a brief hop from Dublin to Birmingham, and our first glimpse of the westernmost tip of Wales looked very like the countryside we had recently left behind. The climate was the same, and the brilliant coloration, but there was, on closer inspection even from a plane, a difference between England and her erstwhile unwilling possession. There was a regimented look here, and many more roads, and, as we neared the industrial midlands, a look of the twentieth century. It seemed dishearteningly like home when we set down at the airport, where nondescript businessmen, briefcases tucked beneath their arms, walked briskly. I missed the shabby but individual look of the Irish, alike only in that every suit looked as if it had been originally purchased for an older and larger brother!

Then our host approached us and bundled us into an automobile, and soon we were fighting our way through a traffic snarl similar to one in downtown Atlanta at quarter past five. He asked if we had had much trouble in Ireland with driving on the left. Britt explained that it had not been too difficult, since most Irishmen walked. The Englishman nodded gravely, "Oh, yes," he agreed, "backward!"

The British attitudes toward humor and history are similar. Both subjects are handled in a casual throwaway manner, yet there is a distinct thaw if the listener responds in an intelligent manner. Thus it was not until we were nearly through luncheon at a restaurant in the heart of industrial Birmingham that our hosts asked if we were at all interested in seeing the green behind the place. It was nothing out of the ordinary, but still – we finally persuaded them to disclose that the smooth expanse of lawn surrounded by a yew hedge so ancient and large that sizeable benches were cut from their depths had been a bowling green constantly in use for the past six hundred years. With relief, we concluded that England *wasn't* just like home, and we were reinforced in this conclusion when we were driven to our lodgings in Welcombe, a hamlet just outside Stratford. We stayed at a hotel which had been a great country house. An enormous place, it was easy to imagine that during the days of its private occupancy, search parties might have been sent to track down Uncle Bertram, last seen two days earlier setting out on a bold expedition to the west wing. Surely there must have been sheepdogs padding faithfully along feudal corridors to round up the farther flung for breakfast.

  All the land hereabouts is known primarily because of its association with Shakespeare – Piping Pebworth, Dancing Marston, Haunted Hillboro, Hungry Grafton, Dodging Exhall, Papist Wexford, Beggarly Broom, and Drunken Bidford – are villages with which the Bard and his companions were intimately associated. His association with Welcombe is well-documented. It was at one time part of the estate of the Clopton family (of whom more will be told later), but the land passed at the time of the first Elizabeth into the possession of John Combe, whose two sons, Thomas and John, were well known to Shakespeare. In 1602 Shakespeare purchased 107 acres of arable land from William and John Combe, and as I followed the footpath from Welcombe into Stratford, I was acutely conscious of walking in old Will's footsteps.

The day was cloudy, but I had learned that England's rains are seldom of the drenching variety. Actually, there was only a bit of faint mist for a brief period during the day. The path led through green fields, and from a thicket the cuckoo repeated his softly mournful chant. The grass was starred with blossoms, and, after I'd unwarily plucked a lovely white spray which turned out to be unquestionably a member of the nettle family, I forewent my lunch to purchase a book on English wildflowers, and identified the other beauties as cuckoo flowers, ground ivy, and water avens.

Shakespeare himself proved a bit more elusive, but I finally tracked him down in spite of considerable commercial roadblocks erected by his townsmen. After fighting my way past scores of souvenir shops, sweet shops, gift shops, etc., I found several buildings preserved with charm and good taste by the Shakespeare Trust. In the substantial building where the writer was born, I saw a summons issued to the writer's father, who had been guilty of dumping trash in a forbidden spot. I also saw Shakespeare's mark – an X – on a lease. A prosperous glove-maker and wool merchant, the elder Shakespeare also served as bailiff, or mayor, of Stratford. Among the other documents preserved here was a playbill from a Ben Jonson production, which listed Will Shakespeare as an actor.

A walk across the fields from the village of Stratford led to Anne Hathaway's cottage (inaccurately named, as the dwelling is a spacious farmhouse).

Char-a-bancs (this is a fancy English name for a tourist bus) came every half-hour or so, and I arrived just after the hostesses had finished one chatty tour of the premises. They were understandably loath to waste all their knowledge on one solitary traveler, so I waited for fifteen minutes or so, seated on the covered garden bench, soaking up some rare English sun, and reflecting on Will's courtship and marriage. Squire Hathaway was a prosperous fellow, and no doubt the villagers thought that young William was making a fine match. To be sure, his intended bride was seven years older than he – twenty-six to his nineteen years, but they must have figured that her dowry would come in handy for a foolhardy fellow who actually planned to make his living writing plays.

Of course, Shakespeare's plots were seldom original, being drawn from history or mythology or well-known folk tales. He also drew heavily on the miseries of the Clopton family for several of his most improbable plays. For instance, Ophelia was modelled after Margaret Clopton, who went mad and drowned herself in a well on the estate. Another unfortunate female in the family, ill of the plague, was buried prematurely – and lives on eternally as Juliet. Still another was, to the scandal of the neighborhood, married several months short of her fourteenth birthday, an occasion also celebrated in "Romeo and Juliet."

Shakespeare was celebrated and successful in his own day, a situation not without its disadvantages, as the only letter extant proved. This missive, from his brother-in-law, asked a loan of thirty pounds. The writer came alive for us with great good humor and beauty when we saw a performance of *A Midsummer Night's Dream* at the Memorial Theatre in Stratford. Along with a packed house – people from Africa, India, Asia, whose accents lilted during the interval – we howled with glee at Bottom, the timeless buffoon, and chortled as Lysander made an unsuccessful pass at Hermia. Will's immortal lines were spoken amidst skillful staging, and the parts of Titania and Oberon were played by so graceful a pair that it would not have surprised me had they suddenly taken wing.

    The most surprising thing to me was the distinct individuality of each section of England from every other. The distances are so small, and when we took a journey considerably shorter than that which Britt traveled each day to get to his place of business, we were utterly unprepared for the striking change of landscape. Left behind were the timbered and plastered structures of the Shakespeare country. We were now suddenly surrounded by the warm, golden-yellow stone which characterized the cottages of the Cotswolds.

    The names of the tiny villages were far longer than their principal streets – Bourton-on-the-Water, Stow-on-the-Wold, and all their hyphenated neighboring settlements. The most remote and tranquil of all was named, incredibly enough, Lower Slaughter. It was difficult to believe, while riding or walking through the Cotswolds, that life here could ever have been violent or even disordered, and indeed, so far as we were able to determine, Britain's exceptionally bloody history did indeed pass the Cotswolds by, and all the hangings, stabbings, and shootings which splatter the history of Albion happened elsewhere.

Within easy driving distance of Welcombe, however, was Warwick Castle, the site of fortifications dating back to the earth wall erected by Ethelfreda, daughter of King Alfred. Here, appropriately enough, was a large collection of armor and armaments. From a suit of thirteenth-century chain armor through crossbows down to an early example of firearms which served as an inspiration to Samuel Colt, the means by which the English have overcome were all there.

One of war's tragic relics was there in another form, too – a veteran with a war-shattered face who served as our guide to the chapel. He gestured with artificial hands toward splendors of stained glass which his blinded eyes would never again see. It seemed strange to us – this constant juxtaposition of Church and Military. We found in every church plaques or statuary commemorating the many victims of England's many wars. Usually they bore inscriptions like "They laid down their lives for their friends," carefully omitting to mention that they did so while killing other people's friends.

But back to Warwick Castle. The title changed families along with the whims of the current monarch, and the splendid condition of the edifice was a testimony to the political shrewdness of the various folk who lived there. The Duke contemporary with Cromwell professed at the proper moment to be disenchanted with royalty, and his successor vowed devotion to the reinstated Stuarts, and so it went. The present inhabitants (and they did actually live in the Castle, although it seemed to me a most uncomfortable and public sort of existence, even if their private apartments were not open to the ever-present gawkers) have held the title since 1769, and several impressive bits of sculpture and paintings of one member of the family by another attested both to the talent and the beauty of their line.

In addition to the armaments, there was a fabulous collection of art, jewelry and memorabilia. There was an ornate golden and green handkerchief which once belonged to Elizabeth I, as well as her saddle and blanket. The original Holbein portrait of her father Henry VIII was there. A mute monument to the cruelty of the age was a tiny suit of armor made for a lame child, a possible claimant to the throne, who was poisoned at the age of eight. We saw, to my relief, the death mask of Cromwell. After all, we were fresh from Ireland, where the natives seemed certain that his evil was immortal.

En route from Stratford to Oxford, we stopped to wander the estate of Blenheim Palace, This vast baroque heap, the ancestral home of Winston Churchill, was built, as the sign surmounting the entrance gate informed us, by "a grateful nation." Begun under the reign of Queen Anne, the palace was presented to John Churchill, first Duke of Marlborough, in appreciation for his military services to the crown, particularly the "famous victory" which Southey describes so ironically in his poem "The Battle of Blenheim."

It was a cool and misty day, and we were quite alone on the grounds. Only herds of placid cattle occasionally wandered past, and it seemed paradoxical indeed that we two should be allowed the freedom of the estate which its architect, Vanbrugh, had been forbidden to enter. The very peacefulness of the surroundings belied the years of controversy which attended its construction. Its first inhabitant is worthy, in terms of human interest, of far more space that I have to devote. Sarah, first Duchess of Marlborough, was a beautiful, determined shrew who made an impact on her times, and this during a period when other highborn ladies stuck strictly to their needlework. She was unusual in other ways, too. During the Restoration, when all of England seemed bent on enough debauchery to atone for the eleven grim and virtuous years of the Cromwellian Commonwealth, Sarah and John married for love and remained passionately, violently in love during the course of their long wedded life. Each of them began life as a commoner, with a small place at the court of Charles II earned them by the loyalty of their families to the monarchy. Each was presumed to be about to make an advantageous match. John had already begun to make his way up in that most worldly of worlds by skillfully eluding the king in the royal mistress's bedchamber. The exact nature of his escape is unknown – some say he leapt from a window on hearing the monarch approach; another less dramatic version has him hiding in a closet. However he effected his escape, the important thing is that the relieved royal mistress presented him with forty thousand pounds as a reward for his quick action. This sum was equivalent to ten times its present value, and the astute John invested it wisely.

John was never a free man with his silver. Even during the height of his fame, he is reliably reported to have left all his i's un-dotted in order to save ink, and it is a matter of record that he refused to allow a lantern to be lighted in his military headquarters unless he had documents to peruse. Both he and Sarah were awed and a bit horrified by the proposed magnificence of Blenheim, and concerned when its design was entrusted to Vanbrugh, who was better known as a dramatist than an architect. To be sure, Christopher Wren occasionally looked over the design, but there is appallingly little evidence that any advice he gave was taken. This is not to say that the castle is lacking in all artistic merit. If the baroque style seems flamboyant, yet it has the virtue of replacing the frigidity of classical design.

    The construction of the castle was interrupted for years, for the Duchess, once Queen Anne's favorite, seemed unable to repress the repugnance which the dull, none too clean, and intellectually contemptible royal lady aroused in her. As a result, the Marlboroughs fell from favor and went to live abroad while Anne's reign drew to its close. As none of Anne's seventeen children survived her, there was a squabble over the succession, with the Stuart pretender and George I, then an obscure German prince, in contention. The Duke and Duchess having wisely sided with George, they were welcomed home to England, where they were greeted with far more enthusiasm than the new king whom they accompanied. So far as George was concerned, the lack of joy at his accession was mutual. He never learned to speak English, or to enjoy life away from Hanover.

    The Duke, a peaceful gentleman of impeccable manners, was an invalid for several years, and died of a third stroke before the castle was finished. He left his duchess the richest woman in the world, and she spent twenty-two more eventful years in that world, during which she quarreled with her two remaining daughters and with almost everybody else as well, while remaining the greatly admired friend of two such different men as Chesterfield and Pope. As for the building of Blenheim, whose eventual cost was three hundred thousand pounds, Sarah fought over every carload of stone, every bushel of lime, every yard of iron railing, every foot of wainscot. She filled sixty-nine sheets of foolscap with the enumeration of every letter from the workmen, the contractors and surveyors, every voucher, every discrepancy, every detail. She fought viciously with Vanbrugh, eventually forcing him to resign his commission; and yet, she, who opposed the plan, hectored the builders and expelled the architect, somehow brought the vast pile to completion in less time and for less money than was stipulated.

    The Duke and Duchess were paradoxes in an age of paradoxes. He was a man who conducted his personal relations with peace and amity, a gentle man who yet found his only real and magnificent métier in the waging of bloody war. She was a beauty who could not control her tongue, nor, indeed, is there any evidence that she made the slightest effort to do so, yet she became a political power in a period when intrigue was the order of the day. Her decisions were almost invariably politically unwise, as in her strong disagreements with Queen Caroline and Robert Walpole, the omnipotent prime minister under George II, yet she gained and held a vast fortune and great prestige. This was a period when the monarchy was composed of dull or even stupid rulers whose subjects flowered with a brilliance never seen before or since. Pope was the poet, Swift and Defoe the political and prose writers beyond compare. Newton dominated the field of thought as completely as Marlborough did the field of action.

Our route led us next to Oxford, where we encountered the only crowded conditions except for London. It was a bit of a shock for us to find that what we had imagined was a quiet college town had become an industrial metropolis, the site of the largest automotive assembly plant in the country and many other businesses unconnected with learning as well. The weather, which had been inoffensively misty for parts of the trip, gave up all pretense of pleasantness, and from the sky gushed forth a real gully-washer, which sent streams of cold water down our coat collars while the wind whistled about the historic towers we felt duty-bound to climb.

Once we recovered from the surprise of seeing that the famous colleges did not rest peacefully in green and tranquil fields, we found that there is more tradition per square foot here than in all the rest of tradition-choked Albion. We were fortunate enough to tag along with a party of foreign students who were being guided through the university by Mr. Peacock, a witty and informative professor who gave his services for the benefit of the English-speaking Union. Like students the world over, our companions seemed considerably more intent on jostling each other into walls, giggling or scoffing or simply getting the damned tour over with than in listening to what Mr. Peacock had to say. Therefore he gave us most of his attention, and in our fascination we soon quite forgot our physical discomfort. At Magdalene (pronounced *maudlin*), which boasts the largest campus of the University, he told of the students of an earlier day, when spirits were less expensive, who loved to toss wine-soaked bits of bread to the deer in the pastures beneath their dormitory windows and then howl with delight at the tipsy cavortings of the animals and at their subsequent hangovers.

The tiny outdoor pulpit, where once a year on St. John's Day, a sermon is preached, is an example of devotion to tradition. This annual rite is observed in accordance with an agreement made seven hundred years ago when the property for the college was given by monks who held John as their patron saint. And because the great-grandparents of present-day students wore evening dress for their examinations, their descendants commemorate their misery by wearing white ties for the same occasion.

Since Oxford's beginnings were clerical, each college has its own chapel. Most of these are rather small, but all are of note, and the chapel at Christchurch contains memorable and colorful stained glass windows. These windows – and others of medieval origin – repay close inspection. Usually amongst the Biblical characters, who are clad in toga-like garments, can be spotted two smaller figures, dressed in the style of the period in which the window was designed. These represent the painter and the patron. Liberties are often taken with the Biblical stories, so that in one window, Eve is shown giving Adam a second apple. Presumably the old boy had decided that he might as well be hanged for a sheep as a lamb, for he is reaching eagerly for the fruit.

Occasionally the morés of later periods caused changes in the windows, so that a somewhat shamefaced Adam glowers in a leopard skin, from one margin of which protrudes the one fig leaf of his original covering! In the same window Eve wears a semi-Victorian frock and a vivid blush as she gazes heavenward.

  The college cherishes a scrap of paper testifying to the fact that Laurence Washington, grandfather of George, left Oxford still owing the University some seventeen shillings and five pence. Once a porter showing some American ladies through the college mentioned this fact and was astounded at the strong reaction of his audience, DAR stalwarts all, who hastily gathered up the requisite funds and pressed them upon him, thus erasing the smirch upon the family name of our founding Father. The disgruntled porter later cursed himself for having failed to point out the interest accrued over several centuries, as well as the change in the value of the currency. This was an oversight he attempted to correct through the assiduous repetition of the story whenever a likely looking bunch of Americans came through.

  I was told that directly across from one part of the campus was a bookshop run by Christopher Robin Milne, but I shunned it. It breaks me all up whenever I read that last chapter of the Winnie the Pooh series where Christopher Robin, having achieved that miserable measure of maturity which made it impossible for him to wander imaginatively any farther with his toy bear, bids Pooh a fond adieu. Facing a completely grown and probably graying bookseller would have undone me completely.

We slept that night in an inn at Dorchester, and it is doubtful if ever anyone had such differing accommodations on two consecutive nights. As I've said, we were put up in manorial style at Welcombe, and all the rooms and ceilings and windows were so enormous that I felt uncomfortably Lilliputian. The Dorchester inn, built in the sixteenth century, appeared to be tailored to the measurements of a nation of midgets, so that even my head, whose least manageable cowlick is only five feet two and a half inches from the floor, had to bow in order to enter our bedroom tucked under the eaves. It was too cold and too rainy for us to do more than glance at our surroundings, and the somewhat harried little barmaid who had left her Saturday night chores in the bar parlor below to escort us upstairs remarked casually that there was no hot water, nor had there been any for three or four days.

Grateful for the warmth and solace of a husband, I hurried into bed. If I had feared that England might not, in the twentieth century, differ enough from the state of Georgia in the United States, I had only to contrast my reaction to the call at our door at seven the next morning. There was a knock, and then a cheerful voice informing us that our bowl of hot water was ready. Now at home, had anyone wakened me with any such stuff on a May morning, I quail to think what my reaction would have been. As it was, we both shouted fervent thanks at once, leaped from the bed to begin our ablutions before the precious liquid should cool, and, a few minutes later, were gratefully beginning our breakfast with a cup of hot tea.

The next day marked our first encounters with two noble British institutions, the National Trust, and the bed and breakfast. The first is a private corporation, founded over sixty years ago, which purchases and maintains the magnificent estates which no family in England can any longer maintain in these days of confiscatory taxes. Their loss is our gain, for the tourist can browse in surroundings of quite incredible beauty and luxury at a cost far less than he or she would pay for a neighborhood movie in the States.

As we drove toward the first National Trust Estate marked on our route, though, we wondered at the extreme ugliness of its name – Stourhead. How strange a title! In Atlanta folks usually name their homes for themselves, but no one had been named Stourhead. We understood better when we arrived and found the estate to be the ancestral home of the founders of the first bank in England, an outstanding family named the Hoares. The house itself was open only on the weekends, but the grounds were ours to stroll, mile after mile of them. There were two lakes, bounded by rolling hills dotted with summer houses and Greek temples and rhododendrons of every hue from white to deepest maroon.

As we looked, I could enjoy the beauty with no taint of envy, for I prefer my gardens small enough to be on speaking terms with every flower and shrub. Here, with the best of intentions and the most willing set of muscles, one could hardly pay a call on each plant biennially. We had not yet become accustomed to the spaciousness of this small island.

Onward to Exeter, where the height and the

grandeur of the cathedral took us by surprise – and so did some of the inscriptions on memorial tablets. One expressed, quite succinctly and in enduring marble, an attitude I had already uncomfortably sensed here. Honoring an eighteenth century spinster lady of philanthropic bent, the memorial recorded that "she displayed an energy of mind seldom found in her sex."

A statue dedicated to the memory of a brave soldier who "died while putting down the mutinous Sepoys" threw me into a rage, possibly because I come, after all, from another colony more successful in its revolt against British rule, and it would rankle me considerably to find a plaque commemorating some fellow who got his while putting the American rebels in their place. On the other hand, it is almost insulting to find no mention at all of the conflict which looms so large in American history books!

As we searched the Salisbury Plain for Stonehenge (pronounced with the accent on the second syllable, please), we found ourselves wishing that the English and the Americans could strike some sort of compromise in their ways of publicizing places of interest. Were Stonehenge located in Virginia, gaudy signboards would begin to shout at the tourist about it while he was still driving through Georgia, four hundred miles south, and they would increase in size and frequency as he approached the site. Now we were irritated at finding no direction whatever toward the mysterious ring of great stones which have stood on the plain for more years than any scholar cares to guess. Finally, in extremely small print, we found it on the map. It was not, as we had thought, near the cathedral in Salisbury, so we missed seeing the most delicately lovely spires in all the island, but, once we had found the ring, we forgave England all her sins. She has exercised magnificent self-control in leaving the surroundings utterly untouched and untenanted, so that the great stones stand tall and massive and as impressive as they were when the Druids (or some earlier tribes perhaps?) erected them to serve as a temple to some now long-forgotten god. Nothing is known for certain about the great stones, save that this shrine must have been of great significance to its builders, who hauled the stones (who knows how?) from a distant part of England and erected them here. One large flat rock is presumed to have been a sacrificial altar; it has been noted that one vista through the gateways frames the rising sun; beyond this all is lost.

    The comfort stations were built underground nearby, which led Britt to wonder irreverently if future visitors, several thousand years from now, might ponder what form of worship occasioned the digging of these cellars. Remembering the identification of early tribes as the vessel bearers or the battle-axe people, I wondered if we might not be known as the pot-squatters.

    We had planned to spend the night at Torquay, but found it the first overcrowded place on our trip. Literally thousands of people walked the beaches, jammed the docks and crowded the shops. We could not determine what had caused the multitudes to gather here, but presumably the weather was usually better than this chilly mist. We drove through as quickly as the traffic would permit, and evening brought us to Brixham, a smaller and quieter village near the sea. It also brought us wonderfully attractive and inexpensive lodgings. The modest sign whispering "Bed and Breakfast" nearly escaped us, and the grounds were so spacious and so well-kept that we thought there must be some mistake. The retired doctor and his wife who welcomed us were reassuring and pleased, we thought, to have some company.

When we expressed enthusiasm at the gardens, the lady of the house took us for a tour of her manicured lawns and beds of primroses, wallflowers, and bluebells. With many an apology for how ill-kempt the place was, she pointed out the palms and other semi-tropical plants abounding here. It was almost impossible for us to believe that we were actually only a short drive, by American standards, from yesterday's freezing rain at Oxford. Callas grew, stately and bridal, as we had last seen them in southern California, and when we retired for the night, we could hear the surf pounding on the shore.

We stayed with Beds and Breakfasts throughout the rest of our trip in England, and if we never found other accommodations quite so luxurious as our first stop, we did find every place meticulously clean, our hosts pleasant and friendly, and the prices incredibly low – an average of about $4.00 per night for bed and breakfast for the two of us. Breakfast was a hearty meal, and somewhat standardized – fruit juice, corn flakes, scrambled eggs, toast, tea, and bacon or sausage, occasionally both, plus broiled tomatoes.

There were sometimes slight disadvantages, too – at the home of a lorry driver in Lynton, our route to the bathroom led down an incredibly precipitous flight of stairs. At a wonderfully picturesque working farm in

Cornwall, we froze upstairs while the family gathered cozily about the telly below, in a room heated nearly to the boiling point. But there were compensations, too – primarily the chance to know people whom we would never have met otherwise. During our luxurious stay at Welcombe, we had encountered only other American tourists, but at a neat gray stone house in Cumberland we found a truly happy man – a geology professor who was spending his days standing ankle-deep in a pipe measuring something-or-other to supplement the usual meager salary accorded one of his intelligence and worth. The New Inn, in Gloucester, where we had planned to stay, was quaint, historic, and served delicious food, but we were grateful there was no room for us, so that we spent the night at a B and B with a flowering apple orchard beneath our window.

    To get back to Brixham, however, we left the next morning, fortified by a good breakfast and bearing a book on the wonders of Dartmouth which our host had forced upon us. We also now knew a beautiful and little-used byway to Plymouth, which led us past an ivy-covered cottage belonging to the gatekeeper of Agatha Christie, over an ancient ferry, and through the first densely wooded areas we had seen in England. There was a mellow, elderly look to the countryside, which made the city of Plymouth a bit of a shock. It was, of course, severely bombed during World War II, and its citizens were rightly proud of the magnificently modern city which had replaced the ruins. They were also more than a bit disgusted with the tourists who tend to pass their sparkling new construction with hardly a glance, as they went on toward the Hoe.

    It was impossible to stand upon this land, a level

grassy park overlooking the ocean, without a tingly feeling up the spine. Here Sir Francis Drake played at bowls while the Armada sailed proudly toward its improbable doom. Here the Puritans bade farewell to their native land and set forth on the first leg of a journey which was to lead them across the waters into a place in history.

From Plymouth we drove the short distance to Buckland Abbey. Although this charming and unusual country home is best known as the retreat and subsequently the prison of Sir Francis Drake, it has so chequered and fascinating a history that it would merit a visit had the old sea-dog never set eyes upon it. The Abbey was founded in 1278 by Amicia, dowager Countess of Devon, for Cistercian monks. In 1336 it was fortified against the French, and for two centuries thereafter pursued a peaceful monastic course.

Then it was seized by Henry VIII and bought by Sir Richard Grenville, the Marshal of Calais. A later and more famous Sir Richard, admiral of the Revenge, remodeled the monastery for a dwelling place, and five years later sold it to Sir Francis Drake.

For Sir Francis there was an unrecognized prophecy of his own land-locked years ahead in the plaster frieze which had been installed in the Great Hall by Grenville. It depicts a soldier with his horse at rest, his armor laid aside, meditating miserably under the tree of life. It is thought that Sir Richard acquired this property originally with the hope of becoming the leader of the Plymouth seamen, but the Queen kept him at home. Sir Francis's principal contribution to the Abbey is the magnificent paneled drawing room. He bought Buckland in 158l, after his voyage around the world had made him a millionaire and the hero of his day. His first wife only lived to enjoy two years as mistress of this manor, and after her death the court lady Elizabeth Sydenham became Lady Drake.

For nearly ten years the Abbey served Sir Francis as a welcome rural retreat from the aggravating affairs of state. Then, in 1539, after his ill-starred expedition to Cadiz, it probably served as his prison. Here his treasures have stayed to honor his memory, and here twelve generations of his descendants have enjoyed the life of country squires in the rich and productive valley of the Tavy.

The tools and crafts exhibited in the Folk Museum at the Abbey serve as reminders that the white-robed Cistercians owned 20,000 acres, which they farmed well, sending their corn, meat and wool down the river highway to be marketed. It was in 1916 that Lady Seaton discovered, beneath the floor of what had been servant's hall, the step of the high altar of the monastery. Painstakingly the chapel was reclaimed, and, after that, the original construction of the Abbey was easily discernible.

Only one other couple, who were accompanied by a too sturdy two-year-old, were viewing the Abbey with us that day. The ringing echoes aroused by his clomping shoes were fascinating to the boy, but although we did our best to reassure the parents that the sound did not disturb us in the least (although it evoked a wave of nostalgia for our own little clomper over the ocean), mama spoiled the fun by removing the lad's shoes. Thereafter he slid about among the ship models, but the thrill was gone.

We very nearly went without lunch, for no eating

places appeared along our route, but finally, about two, we stopped at a pub in Liskeard to beg a sandwich. The proprietor, who drove up to find us hammering at his door,
explained that his place did not open until evening. We must have looked as hungry as we felt, for he relented, asked us in, and while his wife fixed two sandwiches and even supplied two glasses of milk for the crazy Americans who spurned beer, the owner explained the difference between a "free" pub, and those owned by the beer and ale manufacturers. He was a Scotsman who had come South for the weather and had brought his burr along.

    It was surprising to us that, although this is more or less resort country, we found it more difficult to find eating places here than elsewhere in England. Evidently the English traveler rents a cottage and does his own cooking. We had been told to be sure to see Polperro, a quaint little fishing village in Cornwall, but unfortunately, many another tourist had been told the same thing, and we found Polperro, a pretty village clinging to a perpendicular hill, completely covered by tourists and gift shops, and with a carnival atmosphere.

    Fleeing inland a few miles, we had Cornwall blessedly to ourselves again. The narrow roads, too slender for even two emaciated European cars to pass each other, are bordered by rock walls, which are completely covered with a colorful mantle of greenery and spring flowers. The hyacinths, the buttercups, the mint, and the fern tumble over one another in beautiful disorder, and give a look of sameness to the countryside which was nearly our undoing.

So entranced was I with the beauty of our surroundings – it was like travelling through mile after mile of gardens – that I hardly noticed it was getting late, and not a bed and breakfast in sight.

Over all lay such an air of pastoral peace that I wondered how mystery writers like Daphne Du Maurier, Agatha Christie and others came to lay their plots of evil-doing here, where the sun shone softly on farmers plowing their fertile fields and on wheeling white gulls following their wake for the worms turned up by the preparation of the soil. We gratefully followed an arrow indicating that Tremeer Farm, offering Bed and Breakfast, lay half a mile down a rocky lane, and thus found a whitewashed stone farmhouse, its outbuildings nestled close to its side. A garden spilled out its front door like an apronful of color.

Its owners were pleased to see us, their first American guests, and were happy to supply lodging for the night, but supper was another matter. After we had stowed away our luggage in an upstairs bedroom, we listened carefully to a set of detailed and complicated instructions to guide us on the road to Llansallos, where there might be food available for tourists. We must have misunderstood, probably due to the lilting but unintelligible Cornish turn of tongue, for we ended up at Lanteglos, which did not serve supper. We turned around and headed toward Llansallos just as the sun dropped below the horizon.

Abruptly, then, Cornwall showed her other face, the one which leads authors to think in terms of piracy and sudden death. The flower-covered rocks walls bordering the road became, as darkness descended with amazing speed, black confinements through which our path writhed in a vain effort to escape. We finally discovered Llansallos, which offered nothing in the way of refreshment for the weary traveler, and departed for Bodinnick, whence a ferry would carry us across the river to Fowey, if we were not too late in arriving. Bodinnick eluded us for at least twenty terrifying miles, although the map estimated the distance at half that. We spent part of the time fervently wishing that we would encounter another car, the occupants of which might guide us aright, and the greater part wondering what in hell we'd do if we were forced to back up several kilos over this tortuous course in order to let another vehicle pass. It struck us as ironic that we should have survived the flight across the Atlantic only to vanish without a trace in the wilds of Cornwall.

    Hope rose when we saw the lights of a village ahead. Bodinnick? Well, no, Polruan, but at least another set of instructions which led us, in the nick of time, to Bodinnick and the Ferry. We ran, slipping and sliding, down the steep cobblestones to leap aboard. By this time, our tummy rumbles had grown to roars, and we were too famished even to inquire whether the ferry would make a return trip that night. It did, and fortified by a hearty meal, we wound our way back to Tremeer Farm by eleven, and fell into a grateful and exhausted slumber.

    In the morning there was time enough to admire the surroundings – the walls of our room nearly two feet thick, the window glass wavy enough to give a fairylike look of unreality to the green fields and winding streams beyond. In answer to my question, our hostess said that the house was indeed very old, but she seemed embarrassed at the mention of its age, so we pursued the subject no further and followed her husband out to inspect the sturdy and handsome litter of pigs in his sturdy and handsome barn.

There need be no seashore versus mountain debate for the English vacationing family, for here in Cornwall the mountains slope directly into the sea, and what is lost in the way of beaches is more than made up by the drama of these steep cliffs careening into the surf. I imagined that every inlet we passed was Frenchman's Creek.

We visited Restormel Castle that morning, arriving somewhat before the caretaker, whom we had passed earlier cycling through the clear, soft morning. The castle, with its circular stone walls intact but roofless, and its dry moat starred with daisies, resembles nothing so much as the ambitious sandbox project of some giant child who was called away to nap before he could finish.

There were no other tourists about so early in the day, and the gatekeeper seemed pleased to lean contentedly against a low rock wall and tell us of his country's present state. He was not pleased with the state of things. Oh, he liked the National Health well enough, but for the rest, there was a bit too much regimentation, a few too many bureaus, not enough chance for free unfettered individualism, and thus a limited future, he felt, for his sons.

Then onward to Tintagel, where, in spite of such horrors as the Merlin Cafe and King Arthur's Car Park, no evidence whatever has been found to support the legendary connection of the castle with King Arthur.

The earliest reference to this connection is found in the works of Geoffrey of Monmouth, who had a keen imagination and gift for drama, but was not noted for his accuracy! With or without authentic links to the Round Table, Tintagel has greater drama and beauty than any place we saw. Once we left the village itself and followed the path which led first to a small and rugged church, built on land which had been sacred for fourteen hundred years, the centuries seemed to drop away. We followed the path leading to the castle, and flowers sprang from every crevice in the rocks – violets, primroses, the fragrant wild hyacinths which are called blue bells, and then a surprising touch of colorful glory on the sheltered side of the cliffs, a spectacular carpet of rich, rose-colored succulent cactus flowers.

    The region around Tintagel provided a tantalizing glimpse into the life of the people during the Dark Ages. It was frustrating to find that, after the well-documented and extremely civilized communities of the Roman Occupation – approximately 400 AD – there is a period of which nothing is known. Here, on the headland, were the remains of two long rectangular buildings of a type associated with a pastoral people. By 500 AD, St. Juliot, the Celtic missionary, found the headland deserted. Here, with Saint Nectan and St. Keyne, he began to build what became a flourishing community.

    The later stages of the building at Tintagel are marked by some degeneration, thought to have been caused by the Saxon Conquest of East Cornwall early in the ninth century. By the time of the Domesday Survey the monastery had disappeared. It is thought that Earl Reginald, illegitimate son of Henry I, built the first castle here in 1140.

    The Island at Tintagel originally formed a long promontory, but over the centuries the constant pounding of the sea has altered its form and destroyed the very walls of the castle. Now all that remains are the ruins, the winds, the waves, and the imaginations of those who come to view. The stone steps which traversed the cliff were rough-hewn, steep, and slippery from the constant mist, yet we were not surprised to see an ancient fragile clergyman, cane in one hand and folding camp chair in another, doggedly ascending to the very summit. We thought of offering a hand, then reconsidered, for he was, however shakily, navigating it on his own. He came proudly alongside us, and after our accents had betrayed our overseas origin, he assumed quite a proprietary air, and led us over his domain. He remarked how fortunate it was that England, whenever she was in dire straits, seemed to find the leader needed to cope with the situation. There was, he recalled matter-of-factly, Churchill to deal with Hitler, Wellington to put Napoleon in his place (and here he added that his grandfather had fought at the Battle of Waterloo) and Arthur to put down those Saxons. I simply did not have the courage to watch as he descended the treacherous path again, but Britt assured me that he made it, and would probably be returning for one more visit long after we become too feeble to attempt the climb!

    There will be no attempt to chronicle our meals throughout the trip, but luncheon at Tintagel was memorable and deserves recounting. For a tiny price, we had delicious filet mignon, peas delicately touched with mint which the owner gathered from the garden while we guzzled happily at the soup, and a chilled, smooth pot-au-crème for dessert. The proprietor, mint-gatherer, and waiter was a Frenchman, clad in shaggy corduroy trousers, possessing a voice which was a perfect replica of Maurice Chevalier's, and a similar charm. We were early – about noon – and he apologized for his attire, but, as was our usual luck, we were completely free of the plague of fellow-tourists, and the morning marked one of the rare moments when eyes, ears, stomach, and emotions were all content at once.

    It was inevitable that anything following Tintagel should be somewhat anti-climactic, and Clovelly followed. It was actually an entrancing village, whose name meant Closed Valley. It was built on a sheer cliff where an automobile could not possibly maneuver, and even donkeys had trouble. It was picturesque, spotlessly clean, but self-consciously quaint, and its cobblestone walks were littered with tourists. We noted again the hardiness of the British, the number of elderly and crippled folk who struggled down the zig-zagging path, admired the docks, and struggled up again. We noted too that the average English traveler was less loud, less prone to strew garbage, and more appreciative than his colonial cousin. He was jolly, seeming to shuck much of his reticence when he holidayed, and altogether was a lovable species. Nevertheless, we had grown selfishly fond of our solitude and must admit, to our shame, that we did not even make the entire trip down to the docks, but purchased our postcards at a shop halfway down.

    The night was spent at Lynton, a place famous

for what must be the steepest road anywhere in the United Kingdom and very possibly the world. We were fascinated throughout the trip by the road signs – "verges" for shoulders, the promising "diversion ahead" which turned out to be a detour, and the mathematically terrifying "hill – one in three," which meant "hang onto your teeth – the bottom is about to drop out." On one especially sharp drop, we encountered a succession of signs warning, in order, that a hill lay ahead, that it was a one-in-three, that cyclists were advised to dismount, that motorists were advised to place their vehicles in low gear, and finally, in letters of doomsday black, "You Have Been Warned!"

    Here, however, we found something new and different. There were clearly marked escape routes at intervals on the incline. They were sort of driveway affairs ending in a pile of sand, and we could just imagine an impervious British family, hampered but not defeated by an automobile with faulty brakes, manfully starting down the hill, swinging into one escape route for a brief respite, then backing out and heading for the next, and so on down to the bay, where, incidentally, there was very little to see, certainly not enough to warrant this perilous descent.

    The next morning, on our way to Gloucester, we stopped at Arlington Court, a National Trust estate which was a veritable treasury of Victoriana. This was the family home of the Chichesters, whose last representative was a maiden lady with all the instincts of an over-energized pack rat. Since she lived to be a most handsome and imposing octogenarian, she accumulated an incredible amount of stuff, including ship models, stuffed birds, pewter, feather-edged portraits of her ancestors, and gawd-knows-what-else. The carefully culled selection, which was still a formidable pot-pourri, was housed in a beautiful Georgian edifice of elegant proportions. There were over one hundred ship models carved in sheep bone by the French prisoners during the Napoleonic Wars. This seemed to my American palate to be quite the worthiest use to which mutton has been put.

    Back on the road, we were again enthralled by the signs. Masters of taciturnity, the British did not feel called upon to alert the motorist to every single curve – instead, they posted a single "Bends – one and one-half miles," and from there on you were on your own. We liked the elegance of the phrase "No trash tipped," and the suggestiveness of "Lay-by – one-half mile," but our favorite was "road scheme," which preceded a torn-up stretch of pavement. One sign we simply could not comprehend, and this was just as well. Not until we were safely settled at our bed-and-breakfast did a fellow guest inform us that "Road likely to subsidence" meant that there were coal mines directly beneath our path, and the whole business was likely to drop out from under us any moment.

    Sometimes British signs are wonderfully brisk and to the point. At Cleeve Abbey, the National Trust had hung one which I would do well to copy and place in my mirror at home. It remonstrated simply, "Keep your children under control." On the other hand, when delicacy required, the British circumlocution could be a thing of beauty, like the admonition placed in the Men's public lavatories, "Gentlemen are requested to adjust their garments before departing."

Dartmoor came, in spite of my preliminary reading, as a shock. The vastness of it, and the air of desolation, were completely at odds with all we had seen of England. We knew that England, next only to the Netherlands, was the most densely populated country in Europe, and this knowledge could not be accommodated to the seemingly endless miles of deserted moorland rolling past our car window. Actually, the encyclopedia tells me that Dartmoor measures only twenty square miles, but that is considerably farther than the eye can see, and there is a distinct impression that the rough green hummocks, punctuated with clumps of yellow gorse, reach nearly to the end of the world. As memories of Conan Doyle's *B,C* came crowding in, I was grateful that we were merely skirting the edge of the moor, and in broad, sunny, daylight at that. At night, with the wind whistling, it would be only too easy to visualize prisoners escaped from the jail nearby, bewildered suddenly by too much space, too little crowding.

The New Inn in Gloucester was a thriving hostelry some years before Christopher Columbus set out to find what lay on the far side of the sea. Originally established by the monks of the cathedral nearby, the Inn catered to the pilgrimage trade, which was exceedingly large, and profitable enough to pay for many additions to the church building. The goal which they sought, these travelers of the fourteenth century, was the ornate tomb of Edward II, and since the monarch there interred was hardly of saintly character, one searches for other reasons for their trek. Perhaps they were merely appeasing man's inborn hunger for travel, and since the crusades had finally petered out, and long and adventurous journeys to the Holy Land were no longer being scheduled, men had to settle for a jaunt to Gloucester. A less cynical view would credit their pilgrimage to remorse, for, if the recently deceased monarch had been no saint, neither had he been a sufficiently wicked sinner to deserve the horrible death which was his.

The adjectives used to deal with kings are often confusing. For instance, Edward I was generally recognized as a "good" king. He was responsible for certain reforms of the Norman law, which determined guilt or innocence by the ability of the accused to walk over a bed of hot coals and emerge unblistered. Also, it was gratefully remembered that he had conquered once and for all the Welsh raiders, who terrorized the border, and constructed the grim castle of Caernarvon as a symbol of his authority. Here originated the title Prince of Wales, which the king bestowed on his infant son as a sop to the pride of the conquered chieftains, On the debit side for Edward I, however, looms large his capacity for violence, vengeance, and his initiation of the use of the grisly method of drawing and quartering his enemies.

Young Edward II, on the other hand, is pretty universally accepted as a "bad" king, although his chief faults seem to lie in a preference for farming over fighting, and the company of certain courtiers over the affections of his beautiful and imperious wife, Isabelle, of France. Annoyed at his indecision and failure in dealing with the Scots, his people approved when Isabella and her lover Roger de Mortimer forced his deposition in favor of his young son, Edward III. The Britons looked the other way when the former King of

England was then viciously murdered at Berkeley Castle, near Gloucester. Some months later, the rapacious power-grabbing of the Dowaqer Queen and her lover led to the execution of de Mortimer, who was misnamed by the enamored Isabella "gentle Mortimer," and the banishment of the lady herself to Castle Rising, a fortress on the lonely East Anglia marshes. There were rumors that Isabella, only thirty-six years old when she was forced to exchange the gay intrigue-filled life of the court for the solitude of her semi-prison, became subject to spells of depression verging on madness, but these are unsubstantiated by any records of medical attendance. At any rate, she later did quite a bit of traveling throughout England, and on one occasion, at least, celebrated Christmas with her reigning son. She turned most devoutly to religion some years before her death – her last request, made twenty eight years after the murder of her husband, was that she be buried with his heart upon her breast. There were rumors, too, that Edward of Caernarvon had not been killed at Berkeley at all, but, having been warned of trouble, had managed to substitute the body of a porter for his own and escaped to Italy. Though there is some slight circumstantial evidence to support this theory, it is generally believed that the body of the murdered king lies in Gloucester Cathedral.

    The city of Gloucester antedates by many centuries the unfortunate king, for its suffix denotes that it was once the site of a Roman camp. As early as 681 AD, the land on which the cathedral stands was holy ground, and the existing church was built by the Normans in 1089. For nearly five hundred years the cathedral was the monastic Church of St. Peter, until

Henry VIII dissolved the monasteries and the building became one or the first cathedrals of the Church of England.

This is a lofty but cold and gray cathedral. We saw it just at falling dusk, and I scurried past the effigy of the oldest son of William the Duke of Normandy, who died in 1134. Some lingering trace of my childhood belief that such effigies, carved in wood, and lying stiffly atop the monument, were, in reality, the preserved corpses, returned to me with a chill. I was grateful for the warmth and cheer and delicious food served at the New Inn that night.

Our next stop, a resort town ninety-five miles west of London on the Avon River, seemed a strange spot for the discovery of a mighty argument in favor of granting civil rights to all citizens. However, that is what we found in Bath. It was in 1755 that workmen, pulling down a monastic building in order to build a suite of baths for the Duke of Kingston, discovered a number of stone coffins, and, at a lower level, a hot spring. Over the years up until 1924, discoveries were made periodically which disclosed that a Roman settlement of great beauty and scientific dimensions had existed here. Hypocausts had been built by the Romans which channeled the water and to some extent controlled its temperature. In addition, there was sculpture and the remains of tablets, all attesting to the high level of civilization reached by these people as early as the first century before Christ.

They came to England in 55 B.C.E. and remained almost five hundred years, during which time the natives of the land, cave-dwellers of the most rudimentary culture, were exposed to a new and infinitely more comfortable and culturally advanced way of life. Yet when the Romans left Britain, what happened to their teachings? In particular, what happened to the spa they had established at Bath, taking advantage of the only natural hot springs on the island? Professor Haverfield, an authority on the history of this section, says the baths disappeared. Their walls and roofs fell in. The hot springs, still forcing their way upwards, appeared at a higher level and formed new pools; brushwood and water plants overgrew the debris; marsh-fowl came to nest in the wilderness. In short, not only were the Britons too backward to attain any sort of civilization of their own, they lacked even the vision and ability to maintain any vestige of a civilization set up for them and kept in repair for nearly five hundred years. Those of our day who declare the Negro an inferior being because he failed to devise a culture similar to our own in his native Africa must surely also have written off the Britons as hopelessly ignorant and slothful. Where, in the actions of these natives of fifteen hundred years ago – a brief span in man's history – is there an indication of the greatness to come?

"Glastonbury," I muttered to myself as we noted by the map that we were fast approaching it. "There is something terribly interesting about Glastonbury." But alas, I could not for the life of me recall what it was. Our guidebook was no help, merely commenting briefly on a cathedral there, and I was cudgeling my reluctant memory in vain when we came upon a hill – a huge, surprisingly symmetrical hill with a ruined tower of some sort on its summit. "Why," I shouted with glad recognition, "it's Glastonbury Tor!"

"– And?" Britt prompted, as I lapsed into silence again. It was all I could remember, but we eagerly climbed from the car, tackled the little-used footpath, and trudged the five hundred perpendicular feet to the top, bucking a fierce wind which at several points made us drop to our hands and knees in order to continue our ascent. The slope was grassy, and the path petered out entirely about halfway up, and at our destination the small shattered edifice was as anonymous as before. There was not a placard nor a date anywhere, yet our trip was not in vain, for below us lay a glorious view of the surrounding countryside, green and tended in the May sunlight.

By the time we reached a small restaurant a few miles down the road, our curiosity was at a white heat, but the rest of us was chilly, so we paused in hopes of

Glastonbury Tor

a cup of tea and a wealth of information. Our waitress supplied the beverage, and when we remarked, "There must be quite a story about the hill," she replied with great enthusiasm, "Oh yes, the Tor has many a tale..." and bustled off for cream and sugar. It took several more adroit maneuvers on our part before she confessed that she was utterly unfamiliar with the tales.

It was several months, four thousand miles, six encyclopedias and four guidebooks later that I finally found a bit about the Tor in an article in a current magazine. The sea, now fourteen miles away from Glastonbury, once lapped at the foot of the hill, and the island at its foot was believed by the Celts who dwelt nearby to be the Isle of the Dead. To the summit of the Tor were summoned the spirits ready for departure to paradise.

Much later, the first Christian Church in England was founded at the village nearby. Tradition says that its builder was Joseph of Arimathea, who, with eleven anchorites, made cells near the Chalice Well. This well, which now gives 25,000 gallons of water per day, served as a spa since earliest recorded days. Joseph's Church was sixty feet long and twenty-six feet wide, and it was constructed of mud, reeds, and sticks, and all that now remains of it is the Glastonbury thorn, a hawthorn similar in every respect to the plants which form a million hedgerows throughout England, except that it flowers only at Christmas time. The parent plant blooms In the Abbey grounds, with cuttings in the yard of the parish church and the vicarage garden.

When Augustine came to Britain five hundred

years later, he found one spot at least which already knew of the Savior, for Glastonbury's Christian tradition had remained unbroken throughout the Dark Ages. The Wattle Church, as the original structure was called, burned in 1184, and only the wooden image of Mary carved by Joseph was saved. Tradition has it that Arthur and Guinevere are buried in the ruins of the ancient Abbey.

There is also a story, perhaps less fantastic than it appears, that Jesus Himself once came to England. Many years before the birth of Christ, Cornwall was known for its tin mines (Herodotus refers to the tin islands of the north.) Further, it is known that the Roman authorities allowed Joseph of Arimathea to take the body of Jesus for burial, a privilege which, under Hebrew law, would only have been extended to a member of the immediate family. Therefore Joseph, a successful merchant, may also have been the younger brother of Mary. Since the Bible tells us nothing of the years of Christ's life between His confrontation of the priests in the Temple at the age of twelve and the beginning of His preaching nearly twenty years later, it has seemed to some scholars reasonable to hypothesize that during this time He accompanied His uncle on a trip north to the tin mines.

We next drove to Wales, "the little land behind the hills," as Lloyd George called it. My knowledge of the Welsh principally as a nation of sweet singers left me utterly unprepared for the overwhelming feeling of the country – a brooding melancholy. Some of the scenery is lovely – Swallow Falls at Betws-y-coed, for instance, tumbles in cataracts which are startlingly white against the dark rich green of the shrubs which border its shores — but there is much gloom and barrenness. I was aware that there were many sects throughout Wales who expected the end of the world hourly, but there were moments during our tour of the Snowdonia district that I felt these people were behind the times. As we toiled along the winding rocky roads, driving miles without seeing any sign of life save the sturdy sheep who somehow eked out a livelihood from the stony slopes, I was certain that the end of the world had already come, and that we were the only people who had escaped the holocaust. There was a sort of rugged grandeur, to be sure, but I was grateful when we emerged from the mountains.

Wales was a depressed area economically, and it seemed to me that the inhabitants of Llangollen, a pretty village where we stopped for lunch, resented us and probably all the rest of humanity as well. The Welsh language, like the Gaelic to which it is closely related, for the most part appeared to us a haphazard of consonants thrown together with no regard for the necessity for speech. Even the words which looked pronounceable weren't, as in Llangollen, which begins with a "c" sound choking deep in the throat. But the charming country home of the "Two Ladies of Llangollen" was worth a stop. Its builders were a pair of eighteenth century Irish spinsters, daughters of a noble family, who had fled to escape unwelcome marriages, and who for a full half-century after their journey, enticed the great and near-great to their retreat by the sheer force of their personalities and intellect.

Caernarvon had banners flying to welcome Princess Margaret and the Earl of Snowdon, who had come to visit his childhood home, but the smoldering resentment of England erupted for a moment when one of the guards at the Castle told us that here in Wales, Princess Margaret was being welcomed merely as Mrs. Jones! There is a strong, if impractical movement toward independence in this tiny land. For a few moments, we hoped that we might actually catch a glimpse of Mrs. Jones, for there was brisk business afoot in front of the Royal Hotel, and while we filled the car with petrol across the street, I speculated that all the television cameras and microphones being set up could only mean that Margaret was expected. Indeed, a diminutive girl about the size of the Princess drove up, posed for the cameras, had the mikes adjusted to the proper height, and then departed. She was obviously a stand-in, but time did not permit our loitering about to await the star performer.

    Off we went to Colwyn Bay, a spectacularly scenic stretch of coastline dotted with impressive resort hotels. We stopped at one for dinner, and had we not been really ravenous would surely have fled when a formal maître d'hôtel at least seven feet tall asked us dubiously if we were residents. We admitted that we were not, and he hesitated a moment, relented, and then led us to a table. With great hauteur, he presented us with a wine list and asked Britt's choice. When Britt admitted that he knew little of wine, and asked his majesty's guidance in making a selection, I was sure that we would be thrown out immediately, but no – the maître d's glacial reserve melted in a moment. This magnificent creature admitted that he had not personally ever tasted any of the stuff, but he named the vintage most guests preferred, then insisted on moving us to a better table overlooking the bay and the fantastically colorful cliffs which bordered it. All during dinner, he hovered about like a solicitous nanny, and then led us on a guided tour of the gardens before he would allow us to depart.

Alas, we saw no cozy, inexpensive beds and breakfasts in Wales, and were eventually forced to bed down in a hotel in Holywell, accommodations chiefly memorable for their chill and squalor, in a small town sadly remembered for its early and noisy awakening.

The sign at the news vendor's stall, scrawled with grim honesty, announced "Nothing for Holywell Today," a message hardly calculated to send sales soaring, and guaranteed to give any enthusiastic supporter of Madison Avenue instant ulcers. And so we said farewell with no great sorrow to Wales and headed for the north of England, a different place altogether, although relatively few miles separate the two.

As I said at the beginning, our trip was the result of a literary love affair with the British Isles. Most of all, I yearned to see the North Country of England. The introduction to *Rogue Herries*, by Hugh Walpole, gripped my imagination firmly, and because its imagery portrays this land far more accurately than statistics or any words of mine ever could, I'd like to quote it here...

> Over this country, when the giant Eagle flings the shadow of his wing, the land is darkened. So compact is it that the wing covers all its extent in one pause of the flight. The sea breaks on the pale line of the shore; to the Eagle's proud glance waves run in to the foot of

the hills that are like rocks planted in green water.

From Whinlatter to Black Combe the clouds are never still. The Tarns like black unwinking eyes watch their chase, and the colours are laid out in patterns on the rocks and are continually changed. The Eagle can see the shadows rise from their knees at the base of Scafell and Gavel, he can see the black precipitous flanks of the Screes washed with rain and the dark purple hummocks of Borrowdale crags flash suddenly with gold.

So small is the extent of this country that the sweep of the Eagle's wing caresses all of it, but there is no ground in the world more mysterious, no land at once so bare in its nakedness and so rich in its luxury, so warm with sun and so cold with pitiless rain, so gentle and pastoral, so wild and lonely; with sea and lake and river there is always the sound of running water, and its strong people have their feet in the soil and are independent of all men.

During the flight of the Eagle two hundred years are but as a day – and the life of man, as against all odds he pushes toward immortality, is eternal.

We were fortunate to find a sturdy house of gray stone, brightened by the gleam of polished copper indoors, and the glistening of orange wallflowers in the bed by the low stone wall outdoors, and all of it presided over by a most cheerful and immaculate and helpful old lady. We were not her only guests, and after supper we gathered by the fire to talk to a young couple who had escaped their youngsters for the weekend to celebrate a tenth anniversary, and a geologist who was combining the mucky job of measuring the water level inside some pipe with the joys of hiking about the countryside when his work was finished. This is vacation country for the hardier Englishmen, and they can be seen hiking along in a steady rain with monstrous packs upon their backs, or swimming in the lakes when the thermometer measures a chilly forty degrees outside the water and probably several degrees lower beneath the surface. The Englishman has a haughty disdain for the weather, and he can be seen contentedly munching a picnic lunch while seated in a soaking patch of bracken admiring a rain-freckled lake.

    One of our most rewarding afternoons was spent in one of the least promising of places – the rather ramshackle museum at Keswick. The items on display were the usual moth-eaten specimens of British birds, a peculiar musical instrument constructed for the delectation of Queen Victoria, and a scale model of the countryside. The fascination lay in the conversation of the curator, a handsome white-haired gentleman who discoursed of the Lake poets and their relations with the same tone and the same amount of interest usually reserved for eccentric neighbors. For Mr. Southey he had the greatest respect, and he was inclined to look with tolerance upon Mr. de Quincy and Mr. Coleridge's addiction to drugs – both the poor gentlemen had been afflicted with neuralgia, and understandable enough, too, in a climate as damp as this – but for Wordsworth, the poet who had started the Lake Country vogue, he had only scorn. "He and his sister Dorothy, wandering about the woods, muttering to themselves, and his poor neglected wife, Mary Hutchinson that was – of course she was his cousin, too, and probably knew how strange he was when she married him..." He recalled with relish the occasion soon after Wordsworth was named Poet Laureate... "and only because that kind Sir Walter Scott, a grand gentleman he was, too, knew how much Will wanted it, so he asked the Queen to kindly give it to him.... Well, anyway, they called a meeting at the Grange to honor the poet, and the farmers, not knowing what a Poet Laureate was, gathered in hopes of hearing something useful, like a new method of dipping sheep. Imagine their consternation when there on the platform sat Wordsworth, fast asleep and snoring. 'Why,' they said, 'it's only quare Will of Rydal,' and they all filed out and went right back home."

    With some difficulty I dragged him a bit closer to the present and asked if he had known Hugh Walpole. He had, and he knew, too, of his friendship with Virginia Woolf, "but nothing had ever come of it, and those who knew them were never surprised, but Mr. Walpole was ever so distressed when she drowned herself in the Thames." I looked at the original handwritten manuscripts of the Herries books I so admire and would have stayed longer in hopes that a bit of Walpole's literary magic might transfer itself my way, but it was getting late, and time for the museum to close for the day. The curator followed us outside, stood for a while chatting while a colorful chaffinch fluttered about him and finally settled on his shoulder. He explained that he fed the little fellow often, and left to get some crackers for his feathered friend.

Northward into Scotland we drove, and sensed a difference here. Scotland has romance and beauty, but it has also strength and attention to business and a strong self-confidence. Our host, master of a lovely home set in a meadow where pheasants strolled and gigantic hares stopped to stare at us, told us matter-of-factly that the leaders of England came from Scotland and named many a name to prove it. His wife, an American girl and a longtime friend of mine, had adapted happily to life in the small village of Humbie, about forty miles from Edinburgh. Her glowing complexion, her interest in her garden and books and her three sturdy Scots youngsters made her seem right at home. There was only one false note in the symphony – a small conservatory sat squarely in the middle of her front yard. It contained nary a geranium nor heliotrope, but a tiny table and two chairs. Our former southern belle explained that this was a greenhouse for humans, the only spot where she had been completely warm since she came here to live! It was obvious that she considered the chill a small price to pay for so gracious a way of life – the early eighteenth-century home, which was really two houses of equal size built back-to-back, the walled gardens and the brisk, fresh air.

Dinner that night was delicious and the company challenging – a nephew of Aldous Huxley who was a naturalist and a scholar of human nature as well. When we remarked that we had been surprised by the strength of the prejudices encountered in the British

Isles, the dislike of the Welsh for the English, the English for the Irish and vice-versa, the scorn of the Scots for all the other inhabitants of the islands, he answered with a disquieting theory. He believed that the more peoples knew one another, the greater the dislike. The United States, with its tentative amalgamation of Yankee, southerner, westerner, and new immigrant, was merely at the place where the British Isles stood some eight hundred years ago, before they knew one another well enough to be really appalled by bad accents and strange habits.

    Edinburgh was a bustling city whose historic landmarks seemed almost incongruous next to its thriving industries and their inevitable accompaniment of snarled traffic. We encountered the worst jam of all while waiting to cross the bridge which spans the Firth and Forth. Britt has suggested that I might more profitably indulge in research before we visit places of interest rather than after we return home, but I disagree. I'm never quite sure where we'll be going. Suppose, for instance, on this trip, I'd diligently studied up on East Anglia and become quite an authority on the fens, only to discover that they simply would not fit into the schedule. Another, and far more important, reason for listening to guides with a mind blissfully blank of knowledge is that only thus can be avoided some nasty arguments. For instance, a fellow at Edinburgh Castle led us into the tiny chaste chapel of Saint Margaret and told us that she was the queen of Malcolm III and that she died in 1093, after having brought the true Church to Scotland. For this, and other benefactions, the guide continued, she was canonized in 1251. I nodded gravely as I pictured a slender, pale saint. If I had known then what I know now, thanks to a perusal of a biography written by Bishop Turgot, a sympathetic contemporary of the lady, I would undoubtedly have shot back, "Saint, my foot! She was an ugly-tempered hulk of a woman, who forced her ideas of religion on a people who were quite content with those they already had. And she dominated her husband and all six of her sons...etc." I might have added that in place of the gentle soul conjured up by our guide, who trod meekly in sackcloth, Margaret was actually "clad in gowns and jewels more magnificent than ever seen in Scotland." Would the local expert have accepted correction from a foreigner? Would I have been able to keep my knowledge to myself? I doubt both possibilities.

It seemed to us that the primary attribute of the Scots was not their highly publicized thrift — indeed, the hospitality we were shown was unstintingly generous — but their intense pride and ability. Undoubtedly, a certain amount of niggardliness was necessary merely to survive on so sparse a land, a land whose soil has been the cause of what Ian Finley describes as "Highland hemophilia," a disease that has "drained the best Highland blood to invigorate enterprises in every corner of the world but the glens and straths of home."

Another legend went glimmering when we found that golf did not originate here at all, but in Holland. However, it is true that the game was practiced more frequently in Scotland, possibly accounting for the traditional dourness of the Scots' disposition. The famed course at St. Andrews was a distinct disappointment, wedged among asphalt streets and sooty from nearby industry. Less widely known, but more interesting to visit, was the University of St. Andrews.

The Romans, unable to subdue the "savage" tribes of Scotland, built Hadrian's Wall and retired behind it. They had found themselves repelled by fighters whose practice of defense dated back to the dawn of time. The very land has had a monumental task withstanding the onslaught of wind and wave and rain from the West – only immensely hard rock masses could have survived. The proximity of the Gulf Stream is all that saves Scotland from bitter cold, for it is far enough north for the aurora borealis to be clear and bright in its skies. Yet the average temperature is forty degrees in January and fifty-eight degrees in July.

The inhabitants of the land at the time of the Roman occupation were Picts, whose name derived from their custom of painting their bodies. The relics which they left are indicative of a high degree of civilization; they were savage only in being different from their Latin visitors.

The original Scots were Celtic immigrants from Ireland, who arrived in the fifth century. About a hundred years later, St. Columba converted the Pictish king to Christianity, yet the language and the culture of the Celts remained apart from their British neighbors to the south. It was not until the ninth century that Kenneth McAlpin, king of the Scots, succeeded in joining the Pictish and Scottish kingdoms. A century later the land became known as Scotland. Edinburgh, a military bastion named for Edwin of Northumbria, who built the first fortress upon its rock eight hundred years earlier, was chosen the capital city in 1436. After one has delved about in Scottish history for a while, that latter date seems downright modern.

Hundreds of years of bloody border battles were fought between the Scots and the British, culminating in the last great fracas at Flodden Field in 1513, when James IV was king. His granddaughter was Mary Queen of Scots, and her son, James VI, became James I of England after Elizabeth died a virgin.

Although Scotland now has no government separate from England, its law, deriving from the Roman code, is quite different, and its Supreme Civil Court, which dates from 1532, sits in Edinburgh, in the old Parliament House. The impact which the people of this small nation, which occupies a territory smaller than the state of Maine, have had upon the governments and the industries of the world is miraculous. We carried away with us an affection for this land, whose harshness is obscured by the heather and the softness of its ha'ar, the sea mist which can roll in on the clearest day, masking the sun, and blanketing the landscape in impenetrable gray. The barrenness of the soil is belied by the size and agility of its hares, imperious creatures who fear no man. The endurance of the Scots is typified by the disdain with which our host rejected, on even the chilliest of winter nights, the comfort of a hot water bottle in his bed. His American mate recounted with considerable savor his unfortunate predicament on the night when a well-meaning inn provided a china container for warm water in the double bed he was sharing with his mate. With hauteur, he kicked the offending object over to the other side of the bed, where it encountered with some force its twin, shattering both and moistening the mattress.

Wave a phrase like "The Dark Ages" before a mystery buff like me, add the titillating remark that "little is known of this period," and you've got someone who can't resist the Cathedral at Durham, a vast, cold edifice of gray stone standing gaunt and severe on a rocky promontory above the river Wear, "perhaps the most impressive picture of any cathedral in Europe," according to T. G. Jackson, author of *Byzantine and Romanesque Architecture.* Frankly, I found its exterior and its interior bone-chilling, but of great interest as the resting place of the Venerable Bede, that gentle pious scholar to whom we are indebted for *The Ecclesiastical History of the English Nation.* He was a remarkable man who, during a time when most of his fellowmen were bent on forgetting quickly in constant brawling such civilization as four hundred years of Roman rule had foisted upon them, could pen such a simile as this:

> The present life of man, O King, seems to me in comparison of that time which is unknown to us, like to the swift flight of a sparrow through the room wherein you sit at supper in winter, with your commanders and retainers and a good fire in the midst, whilst the storms of rain and snow prevail abroad; the sparrow, I say, flying in at one door and immediately out at another, whilst he is within, is safe from the wintry storm; but after a short space of fair weather, he immediately vanishes out of your sight, into the dark winter from which

he emerged. So this life of man appears of a short space, but of what went before or what is to follow, we are utterly ignorant.

In my gratitude to this wonderful caster of light upon a dark period, I would prefer that if his bones must rest in the dank innards of Durham Cathedral, his soul should forever bask next to "a good fire...safe from the wintry storm."

As we drove toward Nottingham, the fears which had beset me earlier that England had become merely a mechanical monster, its legends, romance, and history smothered in a maze of super-highways and signs urging the consumption of Bovril, returned full force. So far as I could see, no trace of Sherwood Forest remained, and industry ran rampant. We hurried through as quickly as the perimeter roads would permit, headed toward a town somewhat improbably named Ashton-de-la-Zouche, where we hoped to snatch supper.

Dinner at Ashton-de-la-Zouche was probably the nadir of our entire odyssey. Oh, the food itself was inoffensive. It was the company which proved painful. The couple at the next table overheard us talking and eagerly proclaimed themselves to be fellow countrymen. Having lived in England for more than a year, they were anxious to share with us their expert knowledge.

They greeted with a horror faintly smudged with smugness our announcement that we were going, without accommodations reserved in advance, to London on the following day. Didn't we know, they asked with condescension, that the Chelsea Flower

Show was on, and that there would not be a single hotel room in London not already occupied by a fervent gardener?

We had, of course, noted the fanatical worship of flowers throughout the island. People who could not possibly stretch their budget to include a refrigerator were able somehow to purchase a small greenhouse. And it is true that blossoms cooperate so enthusiastically in England that they glow from every possible corner. So well do they flourish out of doors that I was puzzled at first that every tiny village seemed to find it necessary to have a florist's shop as well. At least there were signs emblazoned "Flowers" on at least one building in each hamlet. Alas, I found that these signs had nothing to do with plants. Along with his botany, the Britisher fancies his beer, and "Flowers" is to the English as Miller's High Life is to the USA, an insistently ubiquitous brand.

When we arrived in London, we learned that our informants had been correct. After a terrific hassle with the English pay phone, a dastardly object which required that a button be pushed as well as a coin inserted, Britt was finally connected with an affable voice identifying itself as a traveler's aid sort of person. It regretted that, due to the Flower Show, no rooms were available in London.

"None at all?" Britt asked incredulously. "We do not need a suite, you know. In fact, we've grown quite accustomed to sharing a bath with every other resident on the floor, and it does not matter in the least if the place does not serve meals."

There was a stunned silence at the other end of the phone, then the voice asked weakly, "But you are

Americans, aren't you?"

When Britt assured her that we could survive minus steam heat, private bath, and room service, she apologetically ventured that there were many small hotels in the section near the University and the museums, but she doubted that we would find them acceptable, as they were very quiet and rather far from a store, etc. With great relief, we soon found ourselves established in a tiny hotel which had once been a townhouse. The staff was limited. In fact, one talented gentleman manned the switchboard, answering "Kensington Hotel, heah," with aplomb and melody whilst acting also as reception clerk and occasionally manning the undependable lift.

We were within easy walking distance of the Victoria and Albert and the Natural History Museums, and we enjoyed them immensely. Britt, a fearless man, solved the mysteries of the London underground very quickly, and soon we were miraculously popping up exactly where we wanted to be. We made mistakes, of course, but not on the underground. We took a bus tour of the historic sites of the city, and the combination of our fellow-travelers, whose primary interest appeared to be the condition of their feet and the acquisition of souvenirs, and the guide, who felt obviously that the only way out of utter boredom with his own speech was to insert scurrilous and unfounded innuendos about various historic characters, was sufficient to dim the luster of the Crown Jewels on display at the Tower of London.

And then there was the tragedy of our choice of dinner companions for Tuesday evening. We had half planned to telephone a chance and charming acquaintance we had encountered at the Castle in Edinburgh, a lovely, slender young woman who, with typical reserve, had not spoken while she shared our table at tea until we opened the conversation. She was English and had left her husband and two children behind in London for a brief holiday with the distant cousins to whom she had been evacuated during the War.

    Her husband, she told us, worked for a company which manufactured swords, and when we supposed that this must serve a diminishing market, she explained that every naval officer still required a dress sword. In addition, the firm now manufactured such contemporary items as razor blades. We gathered that her husband dealt primarily with the sword side, and of his recent tasks, the most dramatic had involved a race across the city to the Houses of Parliament, brandishing from the auto window the sword which Prince Philip had left to be cleaned but had forgot to reclaim and which he now needed most desperately in order to open Parliament. When she learned that we were coming to London, our companion had given us her phone number and asked that we call if we had a spare moment from sightseeing.

    It grieves me that the number went uncalled and that we spent, instead, an expensive and unbelievably boring evening with a couple whom we met on that misbegotten sightseeing bus. The feminine half had served with the Red Cross in London during the War, which we mistakenly thought would give her enough savoir faire to avoid being caught in the tourist trap of a restaurant where we ended up. Their names, straight out of Sinclair Lewis, were Henry and Geneva

Ravenhorst and they came from, and seemed to bring along with them, Round Oak, Minnesota. During dinner Britt learned from Henry the intricacies of raising hybrid corn, while I perforce became an authority on the illnesses, terminal and otherwise, of every inhabitant of Round Oak.

We learned after that to bungle our way about London unattended and found, to our delight, that the things we wanted to see held no attraction for most people. For instance, we had the privilege of browsing, completely alone, documents dating from the original Domesday Book compiled for William the Conqueror.

Partly out of gratitude – we were happy with the small, worn, homelike hotel into which the Chelsea Flower Show had crowded us – but mostly because I am a flower fanatic, we went to see the blossoms. Thousands of people had paid a not insignificant sum to wander about the chilly tents, and though the forty-degree weather seemed to seep into the marrow of my bones, it kept the flowers refrigerator-fresh. And never have I seen such colors! Mountains of vivid sweet peas, cerulean delphinium, and one glorious display of digitalis, shading from white to deepest purple, which had me gasping in wonder but which moved one countrywoman behind me to remark to her companion with great disdain, "Will you look what they've got here? Why, it's nowt but foxglove!" Granted that this plant, which we nurture tenderly in the States, grows wild in every pasture in England, yet this remark seemed to express an inexcusable lack of appreciation of beauty, and I waxed pretty vocal about it. I was brought down from my self-righteous perch pretty abruptly the next morning on reading the London

Times. Of all the horticultural magnificence on display, this august journal had singled out the *Passiflora incarnata*, shipped across the Atlantic for the occasion, as the only specimen worthy of a full-page picture. Had I seen it at the Show – and somehow, during the several hours during which I blundered about the tents like a drunken bee I had missed that particular spot – I'd undoubtedly have said, "Why, look, it's a plain old ordinary may-pop!"

It seems fitting to end this journal of our journey with our visit to the quintessence of England, Westminster Abbey. With the corpses of the great tucked underfoot, it was a confusing place. Many who were interred as famous immediately after their deaths have been virtually forgotten, while one builder little-known at the time, whose bones were allowed to rest there only because of his help with the construction of the cathedral, now is better remembered as the writer of *The Canterbury Tales*.

Avarice has been awarded an honored place here in the magnificent tomb of George Villiers, infamous Duke of Buckingham. Yet the true glory of England is here in far greater measure in her poets, her scientists and her statesmen, who have given to the world far more than her number of citizens would ever lead one to expect. Her future? Well, so long as she continues to breed men like the ancient and feeble man who led us about the Abbey, I remain sanguine. When I remarked with joy that Wilberforce, the early advocate of the abolition of slavery, merited a plaque and that not all glory was reserved for warriors, our verger remarked gently, "I think that England will engage in no more wars." When we asked on what he based so hopeful a prediction, he answered, "Well, rugby now draws larger crowds."

England – May-June, 1985

Twenty-three years later, England in May was as green as ever. The haw trees were covered with frothy white blossoms, and the horse chestnuts were incredibly beautiful in flower. We had landed at Gatwick about nine in the morning, and had been met by a representative of the car rental folks who drove us to their office. After a nine hour overnight flight during which we had dozed a bit, jet lag had not yet set in, and we felt alert and ready to take on the challenges of left hand drive and were almost impatient with what seemed to be the excessive instructions for handling the Ford Fiesta which was to carry us for the next three weeks.

A young Indian man with a pleasant manner and an almost blindingly white smile asked if we had reservations for the night and suggested that we had better have lodgings assured before we began our holiday. Sure enough, the first two places which he called for us were already booked; the third had a room on the eighteenth of June, but he insisted that we go in person to check its suitability, for he had never personally visited that Bed and Breakfast and seemed to feel that his personal honor was at stake. Reluctantly, for the green countryside and the haw and chestnuts were calling most persuasively, we found the place, made our reservations, and took off, with the expectation that not more than a four-hour drive lay between Gatwick and Higher Dipford Farm in Somerset.

After almost four hours of driving, however, we had yet to find the highway we sought. We had traveled a bewildering and seemingly identical series of roads through small villages; we had stopped for lunch at a pub in one beautiful and ancient village; but we were beginning to feel that Somerset might be as mythical as Camelot.

    It was about five in the evening when we finally stumbled into the courtyard of Higher Dipford. The farmhouse, 600 years old, was beautiful. Our hostess, Maureen, was out, two attractive girls, sisters Maggie and Annie, told me, but Chris, her husband, came round from the dairy barn to welcome us. He stumped about in mud-caked Wellingtons and did not enter the immaculate house, cordially pointing the way to the circular staircase from the far corner of the living room. The staircase led to a fresh and lovely bedroom and a large bathroom. The design of the quilt and the tablecloth in the bathroom showed sprays of the wildflowers with which we were to become familiar during our travels – campion, forget-me-nots, and bright red poppies. From the bedroom window we could see a flock of sheep grazing beneath apple trees, while from the bathroom we viewed chickens busily pecking about in the yard. Beyond that was a herd of black and white cows, and beyond that acres of pasture to the horizon.

    However harrowing the way there had been, we knew we had landed well, and we dropped onto the bed for a little nap before supper. There was some regret at the urgent need for sleep, as the sun shone brightly and our previous experience with England led us to believe this might the only clear day we might have. However, when we waked at nine for a late dinner, it was still clear and light. We were embarrassed that the other guests, Maggie, Annie, their Mama, and an American couple, had already eaten and were enjoying their post-dessert cheese, but they greeted us understandingly and watched with pleasure as we made our first acquaintance with Higher Dipford cuisine.

Dinner that night began with tender prawns nestled in half an avocado, crusty and delicious pork roast with browned potatoes, four fresh vegetables plus salad, new-baked bread served with their own butter, and rhubarb pie with such light pastry it almost floated off the plate. When we asked where Chris was, Maureen said that this was the busiest time of the year, with pastures to be mown and silage to be made. The days were long, with the sun rising a little past four in the morning and not setting until after ten in the evening, and Chris worked through all the hours of light.

During the week we were there, the sun miraculously shone every day, and the sloping mound of silage beneath black plastic grew reassuringly. Unfortunately, clement weather did not solve all the Fewlins' problems – the government sent a letter while we were there cutting back the amount of milk which they could put on the market, which meant, Maureen told us mournfully, that they must get rid of one of their cows. The Common Market was disastrous for dairy farmers, and only the thriving tourist trade, which had been inaugurated some three years earlier, kept the family financially afloat.

Chris's family had been farmers for generations. His father had begun by working on land owned by descendants of Quaker founder George Fox, but had been dispossessed when the owner decided to turn to farming himself. He had, however, done well enough for himself to be able to buy Higher Dipford, and to be able, over the years, to add more land, so that several pastures across the road were also his. Maureen had come from Wales to Somerset to attend a Hunt Ball, had met Chris and married him. Their only son, James, went to a public (which means private) school, and there was evidence of wealth in the furniture, china, and silverware. I got the feeling that Maureen enjoyed playing at being farmer's wife and looked upon all her chickens and ducks as pets. The hens were free-ranging, which led to some aspects of a treasure hunt in finding their eggs – on one occasion I helped Chris's mother, who lived in a cottage next door, gather fourteen from a nest cunningly hidden in one of the huge and ancient hedgerows. Mrs. Fewlins told me ruefully that the venturesome and hungry hens also made it impossible to keep flower or vegetable gardens.

  There is tragedy omnipresent in farm life, as we saw when the sixteen ducklings hatched while we were there lost half their number on their first night out of doors when rooks or some other predator devoured them. We were reinforced in our plans to grow only vegetables and fruits when we accompanied Chris when he took a calf to market in Taunton. The little fellow, only two weeks old, was so docile and bewildered as he was led into the trailer, and later we saw him join dozens of his mild-eyed fellows in the crowded pens. The bleating of the sheep, the bawling of the calves, the shouts of the auctioneers, and pink piglets nursing at their sow – we didn't need to go to a slaughterhouse to be appalled.

It was a far more pleasant experience to be part of the round-up herders who drove five heifers from the barn where they had spent their lives since birth to a warm meadow for their first glimpse of the world outdoors. The following day, when we went to see how they were getting along, they were contentedly munching the grass, but all came shambling over to see us, and to taste my jacket sleeves and my boots. They evidently felt only friendliness for the species who had imprisoned them for so long.

A before-breakfast walk down the narrow roads, walled in by hedgerows, gave us a tantalizing glimpse through farm gates of the rolling countryside. After a hearty English breakfast – choice of fruit, eggs, bacon, sausage, toast, marmalade, stewed tomatoes and tea – we packed a picnic lunch to the nearby Quantock Hills, a small area covering only 36 square miles but abounding in beauty. Rolling and rounded, the hills are secluded and quiet. We had not yet become accustomed to the fact that a small island with a large population could yet contain seemingly endless acres of solitude. On our hike up the footpath to the top of Cothelstone Hill, we were completely alone with the fields of bluebells and the seven sisters – beech trees of great age – at its summit.

The fields and the meadows of Taunton spread out beneath us. Then we drove to Lydeard Hill, at 1197 feet the third highest of the Quantocks but still considerably lower than the hill our home sits on back in Georgia. Nevertheless, we could see for miles from its height. We asked an elderly couple, the Stephens, who were seated in deck chairs at the overlook, for suggestions as to which of the enticing roads and paths to take. No walkers they, their directions to roadside sights were hardly what we wanted, but it was good to meet them. They congratulated us on the fine weather we seemed to have brought with us and reported sadly that their star-loving son, now living in New Zealand, had not got a single glimpse of the constellations he had missed during his years abroad during a recent three-week stay!

Bluebells

The perilously narrow roads – no need to worry about remembering to stay on the left side when there is only one lane – led through the picture-book villages of Aisholt, Holford, Kilve, West Ouantockshead, Williton, Burster, Minehead, Selworthy, and Nether Stowey, where Coleridge lived for three fruitful years.

We visited the small house where he wrote the *Rhyme of the Ancient Mariner* and learned of the twelve-mile walk he often took to the shore, where he talked with the old sailors.

We drove to the coast, and walked from Bassington two miles to the bay. We were not quite certain what lured Britishers by the thousands to these shores, for the water was far too cold ever to swim in. Further, the sea had receded over the centuries, so that port towns of yesteryear were now landlocked and often deserted villages.

The next day we went to Barrington Gardens, a National Trust site which was quite unattended. We wandered the grounds surrounding the manor house, and at first could find no gardens at all, but later discovered them behind brick walls near the house. The flowers, particularly the iris, were glowingly colorful. The moisture and the cool weather rewarded any gardening effort – there were flowers in every yard, however small.

A neighborhood cricket game was in progress – must have been for hours, to judge by the astronomical figures of the score – in a green field near Barrington, and we stopped to observe for a while.

As Britt attempted to understand the rules of the game, I concentrated on the dogs who watched from the sidelines. One Lab had been trained to leave the ball alone when it was within bounds but to retrieve it when an unruly pitch sent it toward or into a small creek just beyond. It is hard to describe the pure pleasure of simply breathing air like this, so soft and so delicately but pervasively scented with Haw. At least in May, I found it hard to understand how so many of England's sons could have been persuaded to leave her for the far-flung and usually hot reaches of Empire.

It was late in the afternoon when we came to Triscombe Stone, where some foresters were preparing to leave after a day's work. When Britt asked directions, one of them smilingly asked, "Not a local, are you?" The places we savored were not those a bus could reach, and evidently did not appeal to the

Cricket at Barrington

average American tourist – we were the first of our countrymen to be seen thereabouts.

As we started up the footpath to Wills Neck, the man called after us jovially, "Goodbye, Hombre!" The idea that he would have taken Britt for a cowboy amazed us until we realized that several Englishmen so far had remarked on his resemblance to actor James Stewart, who portrayed some cowboys during his lengthy career.

Wills Neck, a name derived from Old English meaning the Ridge of the Welshmen and probably referring to a Celtic tribe who fought the Saxons there, rose 1200 feet. From its summit on the clear day on which we climbed it we could see to the West the distant dark dome of Exmoor, and to the north, across the sheen of the Bristol Channel, the mountains of south Wales. To the south, the land fell steeply away to the tiny village of Bagboroush, where Wordsworth lived for a while.

Meanwhile, we were having a surprisingly busy social life, considering that we were a continent away from home. This was because Alex Horsley, the very pleasant and bright Englishman who had recently moved to Atlanta to be headmaster of the International School and had become a member of our Friends Meeting, had called his brother, a resident and Friend at Taunton, to tell him we were coming his way. When we called the day after we arrived to tell him we were in the vicinity and to get instructions to Friends Meeting the following Sunday, he invited us to dinner, saying that he would mail us a map. The next day Tony Richards, a near neighbor of Higher Dipford, came over to deliver a map to Jefferson Horsley's and invited us for drinks the following evening. He and his wife Allison were very gracious and extremely inquisitive as to how things were at the Bed and Breakfast and Dinner establishment across the street. Maureen, our hostess, being a jovial and outspoken lady, could be clearly heard at their place, and in addition, Allison must have used her sense of smell to pry, too, for she expressed her anxiety to me at the extravagance of Maureen's cuisine ("She cooks the vegetables with butter!")

      We had been touched that Jefferson and Frani, his beautiful, serene, and charming East Indian wife, would take the trouble to invite two strangers to dinner, but we were quite overcome when we found that they had assembled an interesting group of friends to make up a party of ten. Jefferson had, until last year, been a teacher, and most of the guests were former associates in that profession. John and Sheila continued to teach; Gay had given it up to become a gardener, and her husband Dave was a manufacturer. Sara was moving upward to become headmistress of a school in Oxford, and Graham, who was the male invited for her, I think, was a surgeon. Conversation was constant and intellectual, with Graham disagreeing with anything anyone else said, and, in particular, with the opinions of his host. It was a bit of a relief when he was called away to attend to a patient fairly early, after which Jefferson apologized to the guests for the behavior of his tennis partner. "If you think he is rude at dinner," he told us, "you should see him on a tennis court. He plays very well, so I put up with him, although the other day, when he kept some opponents waiting, after they had come all the way from Torquay for the match, I felt I must dress him down and I told him, 'You are an arrogant little prat!'" The conversation thereafter drifted from agnosticism to faith to spiritualism and belief in tarot cards... a very memorable gathering.

We made a return trip to Stourhead, to gardens described in an earlier journal. The varicolored rhododendrons and the azaleas and the lake were as glorious as I remembered them, although I have come, over the intervening years, to a greater appreciation of the natural English countryside and have learned that Stourhead grounds represent the ultimate in management. We had become accustomed, too, to solitude or a few sympathetic souls sharing the spring countryside. We went to another National Trust garden, Court, and while we enjoyed both places, we felt that a walk through what we had come to think of as *our* Somerset countryside was more to our liking.

Nan & rhododendrons at Stourhead

At Friends Meeting in Taunton (where Jefferson

had warned us that the only topics which ever seemed to move the Quakers to speak were early Quaker history and death), a member spoke movingly instead of the anguish and the shame of all England at the behavior of some hoodlums from Liverpool who had begun a fight two hours before the World Cup soccer match between their lads and an Italian team and which ended in 36 deaths. As he deplored the mindless violence, we sympathized but longed to say that the national soul-searching in the wake of the incident seemed to us in itself to be heartening, since a far greater degree of chronic violence had finally come, by custom, to be ignored in the States.

There was an awareness, voiced by almost all the people we meet, of the arrogance and the brutality which characterized the Empire-builders and a gratitude that it was all past. There was almost a relief at being a small and second class nation. As one person put it, "Of course, Maggie Thatcher is equally as heartless as Reagan, but she only has the power to destroy England, while Reagan can destroy the world."

We drove to Brendon in search of an escorted walk across part of Exmoor, but we never quite found the meeting place for the group and instead struck off on our own, taking a footpath from the deep valley at Brendon past thickets of rhododendron growing by a rushing stream, climbing up past pastures to the metropolis of Tappacott, which consisted of one ancient farmhouse and one sagging shed, and onward to Upper Tappacott, a larger farmhouse. We saw no people, save for one elderly couple sitting and savoring their garden in the valley. We discovered the source of the exquisite birdsong which had caressed our ears often – it was a blackbird with a yellow bill pouring his heart out in melody fluid and varied.

Climbing higher, we achieved the moor. It was barren land in early June, and it was difficult for us to understand the attraction which moves the English to drive to the moors, park, haul beach chairs out, set them up, and simply sit, staring at space. In autumn, we were told, the moors were purple with heather. For now, the emptiness was all we could see. Perhaps, for a tight little island like this one, that in itself was a sufficient attraction.

Walking back down to the valley, we stopped at a small inn for a ploughman's lunch, our first taste of what came to be our customary midday meal. It consisted of a large roll, a chunk of Cheddar, lettuce, tomatoes, cucumbers and relish. In this case, there was a certain competitor for the food, which we took to a picnic table, for a large hen flew to the table, perched about six inches from my plate, and eyed it hungrily. I shouted, and she departed.

On a walk at Crowcombe, we traveled across the moor, seeing a brown lizard, the first of his species we had observed here, and found a lair, possibly a fox's. We first followed a line of trees along a farmer's road, then dropped further to eat our picnic lunch beside a stream. A wren, perched on a brush pile, watched us, and other birds darted about in the branches of ancient maple and fir trees. Doves called with repetitive urgency. We followed animal paths with hooved markings and pelleted droppings, probably souvenirs of the red stags known to frequent the area, but possibly only sheep. Wherever there was shade and at the semi-sunny edge of woods, rhododendrons were in full flower. When we returned to where we had parked the car another was parked nearby, and a man stood, one foot resting on the lower board of a fence, simply watching silently and motionlessly the pastoral beauty of sheep feeding in a pasture. It seemed to me that he might know the names of some of the flowers I'd picked, and though I hesitated to break into his reverie, I did ask.

Luck was with me, for Peter Tate of Wales knew and loved the plants well, and was delighted to share his wisdom. The berries, greatly resembling our blueberries, are called Bilberries in England, and whim-berries in Scotland. Hawthorn is also called birds' apple when it is in fruit; tomenil is a plant very like our dry strawberry. The tiny daisies which flower in the grass bloom almost all year round, and the larger Ox-eye daisy is also called Moon-Penny. He thought a bird I described was a Spotted Woodpecker. It turned out that he had also sought lodging at Higher Dipford Farm, but there had been no vacancies. I was sorry, for he and his wife, a lovely lady who waited in the car with their handicapped daughter, were the sort of folks we would have liked to get to know better.

The following day it was time to leave the Fewins and Upper Dipford Farm. It had been a wonderful week, weather-wise and otherwise. The last morning Britt and I faked some pictures of us mucking out the cow barn, Britt chopping impossible-sized chunks of wood, and me gathering eggs. Actually, no such work was expected of guests, and if Annie volunteered for such, it was more to escape listening to the Californian and because she really seemed to love the animals and all the work they required. How we hope that our son Mark will someday be able to arrange a year's work in England and that he will get to be as fond of Maggie and Annie as we are!

    We left with fond recollections of many folks hereabouts, and with amusement at the feud caused when a working farm and suburbia lived side by side. The Fewins' cows, for instance, munched the Richards' newly planted perennials as they were led to the pasture across the road. The trauma of seeing the animal auction on market day in Taunton was somewhat assuaged by our meeting with the Fishers, who had one of the stalls at the market. While we purchased a couple of mugs, Mr. Fisher told us of his two sons and his wife. His political opinions, freely shared, coincided with ours. Except for one young man, an exporter whom we met in Chipping Camden, everyone to whom we spoke was dissatisfied with Maggie Thatcher.

We drove to Cricket-St. Thomas, where the manor house was already a familiar sight, seen and sighed over as the setting for the TV series "To the Manor Born." The house itself was off-limits to visitors, but we were able to get a glimpse of country life beyond the stables where the huge farm horses were kept. The lord of the manor, wearing worn tweeds, led one of the horses up and down the rows of the vegetable bed, while his wife, similarly attired, pushed the plow. Both waved and went on about their business. The rest of the estate was devoted to collection of exotic animals, all well cared for and in such large enclosures that there was nothing zoo-like about the place. Four or five seals frolicked in a large stream, and camels and llamas ambled about in a pasture. There was also a museum of country crafts, and we watched one man fashion with amazing speed a mushroom made of yew trees. I usually can resist tourist-type souvenirs, but I had already succumbed to the mugs and now a toadstool, and we had only been away for a week.

Next we drove to the Swannery, near Abbotsbury. From a herd begun in the fourteenth century, 400 of the graceful creatures are now in residence, and, in June there are many cygnets, fluffy and gray and not at all like ugly ducklings. There are no clipped wings here, and the residence of the birds is totally voluntary, for the profuse growth of their favorite foods in the marshes keeps not only swans, but many other water birds, content with their habitat. Many of the plants along the paths were identified, and I learned that comfrey was curative of arthritis. We made one further stop that day, taking the boat from Pool to Brownsea Island, now owned by the National Trust. The site of the very first Boy Scout field trip, Brownsea had rhododendron thickets, steep cliffs and open fields where numerous friendly rabbits scampered and a few shy deer ventured out as dusk drew in. We saw a red squirrel, once the predominant species in England, now greatly threatened by the introduced gray squirrels. The showiest inhabitants were the peacocks, with males performing splendidly for the admiration of prospective mates. I had not known before that, while the spectacular tail feathers are spread into the huge fan, smaller, but still very showy, brown tail feathers are ruffed out beneath.

Nan at work at Higher Dipford Farm, Somerset

The Swannery

Mother and young at Swannery

By the time we had taken the last boat back to the mainland and had had dinner and driven up the road a way, even the long-lasting English June twilight was beginning to fade into darkness, and we were extraordinarily fortunate to see a sign "Whiteoaks – Bed and Breakfast" in front of a lovely large house. They not only took us in, but supplied us with a large bedroom with an ensuite bath, and we settled in happily for two nights. The following morning we drove to Queen Elizabeth II Park. If at first I thought the second Elizabeth sounded too modern to be of interest, my fears were allayed by the ancient yew trees, with deep woods and paths beckoning inward. I had my first glimpse on this trip of a bright yellow cowslip, now, we hear, a vanishing species.

The high point of the outing was touring an Iron Age Farm in the company of a group of second-graders and their teachers. The children had been well-briefed, and it was bit humbling to have them know more about the time and the customs than we did. The reconstruction of this farm was based on archeological finds, plentiful in this region, and on the writings of Greeks and Romans who had visited here. Also the bodies which had been found, incredibly well-preserved in the peat bogs, often still wore garments whole after 2600 years.

The "blue-dyed Britons" of whom the Romans wrote were actually tattooed, using dye from Woad, a plant common in southern Europe and having this area as the northernmost boundary of its range. The Britons also used St. John's Wort as a source of yellow, and elderberries produced then, as they do today, a deep purple. Gallium Verum, or Lady's Bedstraw, made a pink color.

    The lodgings were of wattle – woven branches and daub, a mixture of clay and manure, the latter being thrown at the former. Contrary to my belief, there was no chimney-like opening in the high roof of the large lodge, for the inhabitants preferred a smoky haze to a fire hazard. Since iron corrodes, relatively few of their implements remain, but enough to recreate the tools they employed in their agriculture, which was of a consistently high quality. Plants grown 10,000 years ago are now being cultivated on the farm, and are of greater nutritional worth than those produced now, which seek stability more than taste. The number of people who lived in rural England was the same – about 5,000,000 – as today. By the late Stone Age – in 4000 B.C. – wood was already being burned for the agricultural value of the ashes.

    At the headquarters of the QE.II Park we saw a film about sheep-farming, which had for centuries been the mainstay of the economy. The film showed in somewhat tedious detail the life of the shepherd, alone with his flock on cold nights of winter, and the Coventry schoolchildren, who had impressed us with their knowledge and interest at the Iron Age Farm, now impressed us anew with their good behavior and quiet attentiveness. Sheep farming eventually become uneconomical, and after World War II skiing and soaring were the preferred uses of the hills.

    There were some pictures of Philip Berry, a World War I veteran who was the last of the solitary shepherds. He was also, we found later, the father of our host at Whiteoaks.

Stone Age village

  After lunch at a pub, with sherry trifle for our sweet, we drove to Butser Hill, site of the film on shepherds we had just seen. It was our first typically English day, moist and misty, as we walked to the summit. Ewes and lambs grazed in the green fields, and a colorful and confident chaffinch hopped quite close so we could admire his plumage.
  Later we went to the great Cathedral at Winchester for Evensong. This structure, begun in the eleventh century, had the usual plaques to the memory of military heroes. One globe-girdling tribute paid homage on a single bronze tablet to the veterans of the Afghan, Zulu, Transvaal, and Egypt campaigns. Ah, those were the good old days, when the sun never set, etc. We also saw a memorial to Jane Austen and later

saw the small yellow house, just outside the Close, where she spent her last years.

Purchasing a few provisions for lunch at Petworth the following day was a real experience. It was necessary to visit several shops — the greengrocers, the bakers and the butchers — in order to accumulate what I needed. At each shop there were queues where housewives waited uncomplainingly and chatted.

As we drove on toward Cambridge, I continued to be charmed by the wording of the signs. "Sale Agreed Upon" conveys a comfortable feeling which a blunt "Sold" sign does not. How marvelous if the States offered a "Public bridleway?" And as we continued to struggle with infinitely narrow roads and left side driving, I composed a verse to honor my very favorite — "The happiest words to see or say are these — a dual carriageway."

We next visited Wakehurst Place Gardens, which are managed by the Royal Botanical Society at Kew. There were many exotics here, and if some were totally new, such as the blue poppies from China, others were startlingly familiar, such as the Polygonum, known to us as False Solomon Seal. The roadside flowers — brilliant red poppies and blue or pink stands of lupine — left me quite breathless.

Speaking of gardens (and I seem to do a lot of that), somehow I failed to describe the most beautiful of them all — Knightshayes, near Taunton. There was a Victorian mansion, in which we had little interest, although we enjoyed our lunch in a restaurant housed in one room, but the spacious rambling grounds were glorious. They ranged from rhododendron-lined paths with stands of foxglove blooming beneath, to water gardens with pools of lilies and reflected rockeries, to formal rose gardens immediately behind the house. We talked to two Swedish landscape architects taking a semester course of work there and complimented their efforts. Down in the valley beneath, we could see the large mills which had been the source of the wealth which supported the house and gardens.

Our choice of diversions was inexplicable to Maureen, our hostess in Somerset, particularly our lack of interest in going to see the South of England Agricultural Show, where the Queen was to be in attendance. We inadvertently drove by the entrance on our way back from Stourhead. I do not know whether it was from an intense interest in cows and pigs or from adoration of their Sovereign, but there was an immense traffic jam, as everyone for miles around drove to the spot.

The road to Cambridge led us through more of London than we had any intention of seeing, and the map showing the circular road was misleading. The circular road changed its name and its direction often, but we gritted our teeth and held on. There were indications, even on the outskirts of the huge city, that values were somewhat different here. For instance, the petrol station where we stopped for fuel and desperately needed directions also sold flowers, and at least every other car we saw held at least one dog. Eventually, we made our way through the morass, and came to Cambridge in late afternoon, eager to meet Robert Noy, our Quaker host. His name was listed among those in England who would host traveling Friends. He had responded to our request that we spend two nights with him very quickly, saying that he would be glad, but adding that there was one small hitch – he had a disintegrating hip and was in line for a replacement. However, so common is this arthritic ailment in wet England that there were hundreds in line for this elective surgery, and it was likely to be Christmas before his turn came up. In any event, he wrote, he had lined up replacements. He assured us that he was mobile, although more so on a bicycle than on foot, that he lived alone, and he gave us further a detailed schedule of the hours when he would be away from home, amounting to four days a week of about six hours each.

We wrote to thank him, and gave him our dates and the phone number where we could be reached at Higher Dipford Farm. He did indeed telephone us there, missing us on the first attempt, reaching us on the second, to ask two questions which were evidently of considerable importance to him. Did we, he wanted to know, prefer brown or white bread? Secondly, did we want salt on the table? He spoke graciously, but a bit pedantically. He was waiting at his doorway when we arrived, a welcoming, well-dressed, elderly sprite of a man, whose gait was surprisingly agile, so that favoring one hip merely gave him a semblance of a skip. He herded us into his small but immaculate home, three rooms down and three rooms up a very steep staircase which he negotiated with less trouble than I. He and Britt got acquainted while I unpacked and freshened up, and when Britt joined me and said that Robert had begun work for the railroad in 1915, I reminded Britt that that was seventy years ago, that he must have misunderstood, that possibly that was the year in which he was born, although it seemed too early a date. Britt, as so often is the case, was correct. Our host had begun work at fourteen, and was now eighty–four.

During dinner, at an excellent restaurant of his choosing, we learned more. Self-educated, Robert was as well read as anyone we had ever known. He had taught himself German in order to get acquainted with Schiller in the original, then took to spending his holidays in Germany. We think there was a romance with a German woman, blighted by World War II, but he continued to visit yearly, and two years ago, even after his hip had begun to be bothersome, he still walked seven miles to his inn, carrying a rucksack, when the bus schedule was uncooperative! When during our stay I remarked on his skill at cooking and general housekeeping, he said matter-of-factly that his wife, who had died six years previously, had for many years before her death been manic-depressive and required constant care. It was a condition probably brought on by the birth of their only child, a daughter with a cleft palate and a harelip. Although the daughter was operated on most successfully, to judge from attractive pictures of her, both as a girl and posing proudly with her groom, the shock had been enough to cause a recurrence of the mental problems which had plagued his wife as an adolescent. He did not dwell at all on this, and was, indeed, as cheerful a soul as we had ever met.

His greatest interest lay in the young patients with whom he worked as volunteer every weekday. He rode his bicycle four miles each way to feed and care for and minister to chronically ill children, most of whom had been abandoned by their families. He also was very active at the Friends' Meeting, which he had joined several years ago.

Inspired by our energetic host, we walked the three miles to and from the campus the following day, finding a bustling city with modern shopping centers, in front of which Cambridge music students played violin duets by Bach, their violin cases open on the sidewalk to receive donations. The tuition at this prestigious institution was only $3000 per year, and even at that 89% of the students were on scholarship. They were a serious lot, too intent on preparing for jobs to indulge in the traditional pranks of climbing the spires of King's Chapel to mount chamber pots thereon.

King's Chapel, begun in the fifteenth century by Henry VI, was very large, ridiculously so for the seventy students who were enrolled at the time of its beginning. Henry had been killed in the Wars of the Roses, but the chapel, containing numerous and spectacular stained-glass windows, had been completed by his successors. There were 38 separate college courts and chapels, and we visited many, pausing in particular at the oldest, Peter.

In the midst of all this antiquity, life did go on, and the young man at the Arms Control table in the inner city was doing a brisk business selling pamphlets and posters. Cambridge alone contributed 1400 members to his group, he told us proudly.

When we followed the sound of band music across the narrow Cam River, with its traditional punts, we found a fête for the benefit of the Kidney Association. It was set up in a field, a small carnival with booths in which one was urged to toss rings, and even a parade of singularly restrained little cheerleading girls. We also met his Worship, the

Cambridge students

Mayor, resplendent in his gold chain of office, and the Mayoress, with her own smaller chain. She greeted us warmly, saying that they knew many Americans, for they often visited American military camps in their area. When I said we were peace people, she effortlessly reversed field and said that many Britons were opposed to the camps and to their missiles. She was even led to agree that security could not be bought by military means and that the funds would be better spent to alleviate poverty and hunger.
Going back through the campus, we visited the Museum, which was filled with treasures – paintings by Lely, Lawrence, van Dyck, and Corot, plus a graphic

pair by Hogarth illustrating Before and After. There were also wonderful collections of porcelain and armor. When we went back to Robert, we learned more about our amazing host. When I admired the yellow sweater he wore, he said that it had developed "bobbles," so he had unraveled it and re-knitted it according to his own pattern. He told us, too, of his assignment, as stationmaster, to greet Princess Margaret. This necessitated the purchase of kid gloves, the left only to be worn, while the right hand was left bare for the royal handshake. One must, he instructed us, look directly at royalty only when being introduced. During the conversation which followed, one should studiously avoid the impropriety of gazing directly into the eyes of a princess.

Robert told us, too, with an endearing skepticism, of a possible ancestor, Farmer Noy, who had been elected to Parliament during the reign of Charles II to represent the "people." He must have been quite effective and therefore annoying to the King, who promoted him away from the people and made him Attorney General. Thereupon he and another official passed the infamous Ship Tax, which discriminated mightily against the people of Cornwall. There was another story about Farmer Noy, which could serve as an explanation for this act of treachery. When entrusted with village funds to buy beer for the Harvest Home Festival, Noy went missing for several days. When he returned without funds or beer, he told a tale of being bewitched by the Little People, who stole the money, of course!

    We went to Meeting at the Friends Meeting House in Jesus Lane, the largest meeting we attended.

The group was quite resigned to being the butt of student humor, which regularly led to the removal of the letter R from the "Friends Meeting House" sign.

Mayor of Cambridge & wife

After Meeting we drove to Yorkshire, finding once again its timeless gray stone walls enclosing green fields where sheep grazed, and where, in the field directly across from the farm where we were staying, there were other feeders as well, countless rabbits who when we approached ran across the field and over a six-foot wall in a veritable snowfall of white tails. There were also three pheasants. The rabbits were not, we were told, native to England, but arrived with William the Conqueror, and multiplied in typical fashion. In what was not one of England's finer moments, the dread disease myxomitosis was introduced with devastating results to decimate the population. Such measures are now strictly against the law. There was a ruined castle beyond this field, with rooks flying above and into its disintegrating roof.

We walked by the Wharfe River, clear and rapid, with mallard mamas and their young forming flotillas. I did not know much about duck family life, and so I wondered where the colorful fathers were. We saw one trio of males having a carefree stag party in a small stream at Malham the following day, with no responsibilities at all.

We have run out of superlatives to describe the English countryside in May, but Britt and I are agreed that the Wharfedale area is the loveliest of all. We found a sturdy stone bridge now leading nowhere on either side, with stepping stones alongside which must have predated its long-ago construction. Next day we drove to the Malham area, where we hiked to Janet's Cave and her fosse (waterfall). Janet was queen of the fairies of the place, and it was customary to leave offerings of food and flowers at her cave entrance to keep in her good graces.

Next we walked to Goredale Scar, a rocky, glacier-scoured deep valley, and then on to Malham Cove. On the way, we encountered several times the ultimate English dog-lover. Everywhere in Yorkshire there were high rock walls separating the fields, and they had to be climbed over via stiles. Climbing stiles was beyond a dog's ability, evidently, for we saw hikers lifting, with much effort, heavy labs over the stiles. One couple, who had his and her fat dogs to lift, told

Yorkshire

that one had suffered from some ailment, unfamiliar to us, so serious that their vet had advised putting it down, since it would never make much of a dog anyhow, and the only known treatment was very demanding. Scorning his advice, they had slept only in shifts for several days while administering two teaspoons of water every fifteen minutes around the clock. It had been a cure, and so healthy did the dog seem now that we were amazed the owner had not sprung a hernia from hauling the monster over stiles. A few minutes later, we achieved our last steps of the day – for me they would be the last steps for a long, long time.

Our guidebook described a "greeny white amphitheatre formed by the cliffs of Malham Cove." At the top strange rock formations created a vast waffle-life area of rock, the edge ending abruptly in a sheer face used by rock climbers from below and suicides from above.

Yorkshire

Until shortly before, there had been a steep path for those who preferred neither, but it had begun to erode, so a stair of sorts had been built, but with no handrail and steps of uneven height covered with loose rock. All this description is by way of alibi for the fact that, although I exercised extreme caution and managed to negotiate the first hundred steps or so with only one harmless turn of an ankle, I hit a very recalcitrant rock about ten steps from the end and broke my right ankle on both sides. Loudly disdaining Britt's urgent offer to carry me to the foot of the stairs, I bumped my way down on my bottom and waited for him to go to find help. An Australian lady doctor who fortuitously came hiking by pronounced the ankle badly broken and cautioned me not to move at all, for fear of

Stone Bridge

compounding the mess. Britt meanwhile walked to the nearest phone, a couple of miles away, called the police, explained the situation and asked that they send a four-wheel drive with a stretcher and men to handle it. After some time a pleasant, rosy-cheeked young Yorkshireman arrived with none of the above. He drove his police car as far as he could before rocks made further entry perilous, and then began to walk with Britt back to where I sat.

    By then the doctor had climbed to the Cove and descended again, and she waited with me. The policeman, after they had walked half a mile, asked Britt with some concern, "Tell me, sir, is your wife a

Janet's Fosse, Yorkshire

large woman?" Although Britt assured him that I was not, it is probable that I'd still be sprawled among the rocks if Britt had not once been a Boy Scout who recalled the crossed hands carry. The policeman carried his half the whole way, while Britt and two others took turns with the other half. As the policeman loaded me into his car, he rubbed his chafed wrists ruefully and said, "I'm glad you're no heavier, luv!"

Airedale Hospital received me graciously, the ankle was set by about nine in the evening, and they even provided a room, free, and pajamas for Britt to spend the night. The following morning I spent on the phone searching out a wheelchair, and we drove to the Red Cross in Leeds to pick it up. We had to stay in the area for four days to have the surgeon check the ankle again, but we had planned to stay in Yorkshire anyway.

Back we drove to the picturesque but primitive farmhouse where we had spent one night before the accident. Among the other guests were now a Swedish family, the wife an archeologist. They highly recommended a visit to the Viking Museum in York, so the next morning, which was overcast and boasted a piercing wind, we took off for York.

The Museum was worth the trip. One sat in a small car and was propelled backward through time past the medieval villages and the Norman invasion, the latter complete with the smell of the fires as the Normans burned all that lay in their way. The virtual tour finally led to a bustling market town with dark, smoky houses and a busy wharf – all recreated just as they were. The detail was accurate, for archeologists had discovered, adjacent to this reconstruction, complete houses and workshops. They still contained the utensils, the tools, and even the clothing of a civilization which had lain buried for a thousand years. After seeing the reconstruction, the car took one, so smoothly and silently that it has to be powered by magnets, to the archeological dig itself, and then to the artifacts hall, where we saw the magnificent and delicate objects found on the dig. It was quite unforgettable.

Afterwards we went on a journey we both wish we *could* forget. It is impolite to criticize a free wheelchair, but the one the British Red Cross made available for us had seen many a ride, and the cobbled streets of York nearly did it and us in. We were searching for the Minster, the huge church which overshadows the whole town, but we found its base remarkably and infuriatingly elusive. The wind was "lazy" – that is, as a fellow lodger at our farm near Skipton told us, "It is too lazy to go around you, and so it goes right through instead." I had borrowed from our farm a blanket which had seemed small on the bed but proved much too large to serve as a lap robe. No matter how carefully we wrapped it around me, it kept coming loose and entangling itself in the wheels. Our way was further complicated by the front tire, which came off the wheel three times, necessitating Britt's hailing a passing stranger and asking him to balance me and my chair on the two back wheels while he re-affixed the tire to the front left one.

Eventually we made our way to York Minster, which was old and large and filled with tourists. Its construction was begun in Saxon times, well before 1066, and that's about all I remember. I was so preoccupied with wondering whether the wheelchair and I would survive the return trip to the car that I was not too alert an observer. I persuaded Britt to park me at the rear of the church while he went back to the car and sought some way to drive near enough to pick me up. The warden to whom we explained the situation agreed to keep an eye on me, but he became more and more nervous as the minutes ticked by and Britt did not return. I knew well the problems my husband would be encountering trying to thread his way through the narrow clogged streets, many marked off-limits to motor vehicles and others one-way, always in the wrong direction. Eventually I was reclaimed, and we

Bed & Breakfast, Yorkshire

drove back to the farm, to liver for dinner. This, along with the steepness of the stairs and the antiquity of the bath (a single one shared with the family and other guests) impelled us to search out another farm, whose praises had been enthusiastically sung by a lady whom I'd met while we were touring Bolton Priory two days earlier.

It turned out to be a very wise move, to charming quarters. Although Heather, our hostess, did not offer dinner, our fellow guests Derek and Ann recommended a restaurant nearby and escorted us there. The food and the view and the company were all great, and we made a return trip the following evening. Britt had pronounced the shrimp scampi about the most delicious morsels ever to tickle his palate, and the second night I tried them and concurred. Our companions, too, were most enjoyable. Derek worked for the telephone company and was a humorous and helpful fellow. At some point during our first dinner, Britt had asked if he had any heroes or heroines. He matter-of-factly pointed to Ann, and, as we came to know her better, we understood why. Their own two children were now in their twenties and on their own, and Ann worked as buyer for a large garden center. Previously, when their children were small, she had stayed home with them and contributed to the family income by providing care for other children as well. Many of these were charity cases, and she spoke of all her charges with such perception and love that we knew she must have made a great difference in many young lives.

     My sharpest recollection of the Simpkins' lovely home was of the Rotweilers who guarded the place during the day while Heather was at work at a farm supply store and her husband was performing the endless chores of a dairy farmer. One dog stayed shut up in a shed in the barn, where he alternately groaned and growled at passersby. The mother was kept confined in the family part of the house except during the hours of ten to four during the day, when guests were banished and she roamed throughout the house to keep guard. On one occasion she was not shut away when I entered the kitchen, crutches swinging wildly. She looked distinctly uneasy, as any reasonable dog would, and I asked Heather's daughter to bring the dog in to meet me under less threatening circumstances, when I was seated and the crutches were out of sight. She agreed and brought the hulking creature in.

She came up and sniffed me amiably enough, but when I reached out to pat her, the girl cautioned, "I wouldn't come too close. She's funny." When I finally asked her to spell that last word, after repetition had not made it any more comprehensible, she complied,

"F U N N Y."

"What does that mean?"

She thought a moment and ventured, "Unreliable."

"Has she ever actually bitten anyone?" I persevered, and she explained that yes, the dog had once bitten her on the face but only, she qualified, because she had taken its bowl away. The bowl had been empty, but the dog had not been ready to give it up. On another occasion the dog had bitten her sister, nobody was sure why, although there must have been some reasonable excuse. I decided to keep my distance.

The Yorkshire accent, when used between two natives, was quite incomprehensible to our ears, though when they spoke to us our hosts must have made a conscious effort to be clear, for we could understand them then well enough. At the hospital, we had noted that the higher the level of education, the less Yorkshire there was in the mouth. It was clear that the locals' ability to comprehend us varied, too, for the porter who met us when we first arrived at the hospital asked me, "Tell me, is your husband Welsh? I can't understand a word he says." The wife of the Anglican Bishop of Glasgow, a lovely lady with diabetes, came by my room to visit. She spoke beautifully, in a way I'd love to be able to imitate, and said she had come to Airedale Hospital for treatment because they were so welcoming and kind. We concurred and wondered if they might even be a touch masochistic, since they proffered tea at least six times daily to a lot of bedridden patients, which must have resulted in numerous calls for bedpans!

While seeing the unbelievably lovely land in Yorkshire, we learned more about its history. Britt had always suffered from knowing that the first known Pendergast was one Maurice, who accompanied William the Conqueror on his invasion of England in 1066. We knew he had beaten the Saxons under Harold at the Battle of Hastings, and Britt had always felt that it was hardly a fair fight, since Harold was also engaged in fending off invading Vikings.

Now we have found out a bit more about the encounter and the events which led up to it, and while it is hardly possible to view Maurice and his leader as peaceful visitors, there were certain extenuating circumstances. Edward the Confessor, later canonized, had been an exemplary Christian who felt called upon to expel all the Jews from England. When he died without successor, William of Normandy expected to inherit the English throne – after all, Edward had spent much of his time in Normandy, and had on many occasions promised that William the Bastard was his chosen heir. When Edward left the throne instead to Harold, William was sure that pressure had been brought to bear and made plans to claim the throne. To this end he persuaded the Pope to recognize his claim and the Vikings to invade. The Normans of the time were Norsemen, not Frenchmen, and it is probable the Vikings were cousins of sorts.

We also learned that William had been a fervent, if somewhat unsubtle, suitor to one Matilda. When she refused his suit, he proceeded to kick her and then drag her about the room by her braids. She found this persuasive, but she had to call him back in order to accept, since after hauling her about by her hair he had left hurriedly.

The Normans settled in, and William distributed the choice lands to his followers. Among them, the Percy family was granted a large and lovely chunk of what is now Yorkshire. Subsequently they built large churches to assure the health of their souls, one of these being the priory at Bolton. Actually, it was never an Abbey at all, but rather a small religious house of the Augustinian order. Originally established by Alice de Romilly and her son William at Embsay in 1120, it was moved in 1154 to its present site, surrounded by flat fields near the Wharfe River, with bracken and heather-covered fells rising gently beyond. Although the priory itself was in picturesque ruins, we found that life went on largely unchanged. A shepherd with his dog drove a flock of sheep from one pasture to another, seemingly undisturbed by a Lab who rushed up wanting to play and who paid no attention to the frantic shouts of his master, who had another Lab on a leash. When the playful Lab finally returned and his master walked on toward us, we asked if the dog had ever injured any sheep. "Oh, no," he laughed, "but occasionally during lambing season a ewe has attacked him. One would think that he would learn."

While I patted the other dog, a tranquil soul, he told us that she was not actually his. An elderly neighboring couple had lost their dog, and when this one had shown up, he had given her to them. He obviously walked the dog every day for them. The tale sounded like the stuff of Herriot chapters.

It was wonderful to know that this area of the Yorkshire Dales was now a property of the National Trust, and would remain forever a peaceful, chilly Eden of pastures with grazing cattle and sheep, clear rivers rippling, and above it all a constantly shifting cloud pattern. It may rain and clear half a dozen times a day. Farmers and English holidaymakers alike carry rain gear constantly. As enjoyable as the surroundings are the people who live here. Their way of expressing themselves enchants us – for instance, John, a fellow lodger at Heather and Bill Simpson's, described a particularly rough wine as such that, had it been taken to a chemist for analysis, one would have been advised to take the animal that produced it to a vet.

Their humor was understated and effortless and present under the most difficult of circumstances, so that a 6'6" outpatient at Airedale Hospital, in for a checkup for a back ailment, discovered that he should have brought his pajamas. He refused his wife's offer to return to their home to bring some, although she told us he hated hospital gowns. As we were leaving, he emerged from a waiting room, clad in the offending garment, to wish us farewell. He did indeed look foolish, with a length of leg at least as long as all of me protruding.

Britt said, "They have pajamas here, for they

lent me a pair."

He answered quickly, "Ah, but that's it. They only have one pair and they save it for Americans." American influence extended beyond commandeering pajamas, too. American music seemed to permeate the airwaves – we heard a station broadcasting from St. David's in Wales offer "Somebody Stole My Gal," and "Shortnin' Bread."

We drove to the Lake District the following day. This relatively small, but incredibly beautiful, area was, until the nineteenth century, what the poet Gray described as "this little unsuspected paradise." A succession of blue, blue lakes, the product of the last great ice age when countless glaciers advanced and retreated over a million years, are bordered by England's highest mountains. The whole picture is somewhat in miniature, for Scafell Pike is only 3206 feet in altitude, but the effect is one of grandeur. Rhododendron flowers profusely at the bases of the fells, and along the valley roadsides are purple geranium, yellow poppies, and blue speedwell. At Ullswater Lake there is a fairly wide valley where sheep graze in a field dotted with Queen Anne's Lace and golden buttercups.

Although the average Briton might not have been aware of the Lake District until the 1800's, artifacts show the region to have been inhabited for thousands of years. Little is known of the earliest settlers here, but the people of the Bronze Age built villages on the fells, avoiding the boggy areas around the lakes. The region was strategically important to the Romans because of its proximity to Hadrian's Wall. Later came the Norsemen and still later, Wordsworth, whose poetry made the Lake District the foremost tourist spot in the country.

My first awareness of the lake district had come from the writings of Hugh Walpole, whose novels of the Herries family begin with this description – "There is no ground in the world more mysterious, no land at once so bare in its naturalness and so rich in its luxury, so warm with sun and so cold in pitiless rain, so gentle and pastoral, so wild and lonely; with sea and lake and river there is always the sound of running water, and its strong people have their feet in the soil and are independent of all men." We had visited here twenty-three years ago and found his description apt.

Our first look this time was disturbing, for Windermere, the first lake we encountered, was now totally surrounded with tourist lodges, and its shores quite covered with elderly, grim faced tourists. We found, however, as we penetrated deeper into the district that the tourists, as was their blessed wont, tended to congregate, and at Cat's Bells, where Walpole had his cottage, total solitude and the wildness of which he wrote prevailed.

On the way back to our lodgings near Skipton, we saw tinker caravans parked by the road, and a little up the way the tinkers themselves (the British term for gypsies, because of their work as repairers of pots and pans.) We had read that now, with new utensils bought instead of old ones repaired, the tinkers were having a difficult time eking out a livelihood, but we were relieved to see that the men, wearing their distinctive black felt hats, were grazing horses who looked well fed, and that they themselves were gathered from all over England for the annual horse fair. That evening marked our second dinner at Tarn House with Derek and Ann Soanes. In the course of two shared teas and two leisurely dinners, we learned more about them than we knew of many of our neighbors of thirty years. Our next and last stop was the Cotswolds. This, too, was a longer visit to an area we had met and loved on our earlier trip. The golden stone on which the land lies seems, as J. B. Priestly put it, "to keep the lost sunlight of centuries glimmering upon them." I am aware that I used a lot of superlatives on the Lake District, but a whole new set is called for here. This was a tended land of thatched cottages and

Lake Windermere

manicured gardens, of small shops and gentle people. This was a culture built upon wool. "Cots" is from the old Saxon word for sheepfold, and "wolds" describes high open land. The wool merchants who thrived here built manor houses and churches. By the end of the eighteenth century, the West Country wool and cloth trade had begun to decline, superseded by the coal-powered mills of Lancashire and Yorkshire, but the glories of the past survived in such places as Chipping Campden, called simply Campden by its residents, partly for the sake of abbreviation and possibly because the original meaning of Chipping was cheap. The word surely did not apply to our overwhelmingly generous hostess, Quaker Katharine Gell. When we wrote to her, having found her name in the list of those Britons who volunteer to take traveling Quakers as guests, we thought we would stay in the Rose Cottage, where she lived, but on arrival were told that reservations had been made – and paid for, it turned out – at the inn in the village. Knowing in advance of my broken ankle, she had reserved not only a ground-floor, spacious sunny bedroom, where she had placed bowls of fresh fruit and flowers and stacks of literature about the area, but had even found a wheelchair.

We settled in gratefully for a few minutes, then sought out Rose Cottage, where we knew the gardens were on display for charity.

We found Katharine a large, bluff hearty woman of strong opinions, with most of which, fortunately, we concurred. She had for years served as the super-secretary at Blenheim Castle, the huge castle where Winston Churchill was born, but did not stay. Present residents were his cousin, the Duke of Marlborough, whom our hostess described as "dim," and his wife, of whom she took a slightly more charitable view. I am certain that she did a tremendously efficient and overpowering job of running the Castle, and suspect that the Duke and Duchess might have been relieved when she retired to do volunteer work and spend her considerable inherited wealth on worthy causes. When our host at the inn told us that Katharine had already paid our bill there, Britt suggested that we pay him, too, and that he explain to Katharine. He blanched and begged off. "She would," he said, "simply tear your check into hun--dreds of pieces and throw them at me." We settled for sending a cheque for the same amount to Katharine, asking that she donate it to

Tinkers

Rose Cottage, Lower Slaughter

St. John's Ambulance Society or the Broader Campden Friends Meeting. We did not receive the tattered shreds of the cheque in the mail, so presumably it was acceptable.

    Katharine did agree to allow us to take her to dinner one evening, and on the following one, she had us to a catered dinner at her charming cottage, made of the mellow golden stone, with a huge fireplace, so comfortable and cared for that it was hard to believe it was three hundred years old.

    The birdsong here seemed unusually melodic, possibly because of its unfamiliarity. The Britons are enthusiastic birdwatchers, with some 500,000 members of bird societies. Among the feathered fellows we admired were black and white wagtails, green finches (who are yellow), chaffinches, gulls, curlews, and wrens, in addition to the yellow–billed blackbirds, whose song I mentioned earlier.

    We learned much about the origin of Campden from Katharine. It is very old indeed, having been mentioned in the Domesday Book commissioned by William the Conqueror. It seems likely that its name was derived from the graveyard established after the last battle between Saxons and Britons, about the year 690. We went to the Church at Chipping Campden, the parish church of Berrington, and wandered the length of the High Street, on which our inn was situated. It seemed incredible to us that the place remained, after all the centuries of habitation, so beautiful and so cared for. It must be that in a country so small the frontier philosophy which seems yet to motivate Americans (although the frontier is long since conquered) is missing. We never saw in Europe a tendency to trash the place and move on.

    We had watched no television in England until our last two evenings, and we found then that the nightly news differs from ours. In a half-hour segment, for instance, there were three stories which would never, we think, be found wedged between American commercials for hemorrhoid relief and mouthwash – the Queen and Prince Phillip welcoming, with much pomp and pageantry, the President of Mexico, the Prince and Princess of Wales attending a charity premiere of the latest James Bond film, and the Lord Mayor of London ceremonially ringing the bells of Old Bailey for the first time in thirty years. None of these activities in any way solved the very real problems facing England and the planet, but they were somehow comfortable nonetheless.

We now visited Hidcote Garden, a National Trust site begun in 1905 by a retired military officer who saw in a nondescript hillside deep in the Cotswolds the possibility of acres of glorious gardens. They were built on several levels, and Britt managed to bump me and the wheelchair down to almost all of them and back up again. We encountered a couple from Yorkshire who said they knew Malham Cove, the site of my disaster, well, for their son had often engaged in rock-climbing there. When I said I hoped he had come to his senses and quit, as had our son Scott, they said "Hardly. He moved on to higher places, and last year was part of the Everest expedition which was forced to turn back when its leader suffered a heart attack!" It made us grateful that Scott moved on to kayaking wild rivers.

Broader Campden Friends Meeting, which we attended, was probably the oldest in the world, dating back to 1683 (I think). A simple but beautiful building made of that golden rock, the meeting house was surrounded by countryside, so that the only sounds during the silent meeting were doves cooing and the bleat of a lamb on a distant but visible hillside.

The beginnings were not so tranquil – Quakers were once sentenced to the stocks for walking through the village on Sunday. A Quaker was also punished for rising on two occasions to speak after the sermon. He was let off with a warning the first time he tried to fill in the gaps left by the Anglican minister, but when he committed the same offense the following Sunday, he was put in jail.

Now it was time to leave England, and for the first time after a three-week holiday (our maximum absence from home and family) we were not eager to depart. In spite of my ankle, it had been a wonderful holiday, the sort that sets one to dreaming of return. Perhaps next time we could see Hadrian's Wall and the Highlands of Scotland. Perhaps we might even venture across the Channel to Normandy....

England – Spring, 1999

After leaving Atlanta at a respectable 5:30 pm, we flew for about eight hours, were awakened at what felt like 1:30 the following morning, were fed a hearty English breakfast and disembarked, groggy but hopeful. Daylight had arrived in England. We picked up our small rental car and drove off on the wrong side of the road like everyone else. Unsurprisingly, it was raining, and, also unsurprisingly, the Brits were ignoring it. They were playing tennis in the wet, and equestrians were riding unconcernedly along country roads not wide enough for two very small cars to pass each other. The only concession to the weather was that the plastic covers on prams were raised, and infants smiled or drowsed contentedly beneath them. During our stay we never saw an unhappy child.

We stopped at Thacham on the way to our destination, Bradford-on-Avon, to cash travellers cheques and were at first bewildered when the cashier directed us to the Lloyds' across the street, explaining that they would give us better rates. Capitalism here was not of the unbridled American variety.

We had been to Stonehenge on two previous occasions and had been disappointed to find on the second trip that a busy highway had been cut very close to the mysterious rocks, and that a fence topped by barbed wire was even closer. This time we headed for Avebury, an undisturbed village built among a ring of stones 360 feet in diameter, surrounded by a ditch which was now only about thirteen feet deep but which had once been far deeper, since seventeen feet of silt had accumulated over the centuries since it was constructed. The religious architecture of the Beaker and Bronze Age people is our most spectacular legacy of the prehistoric inhabitants of this area. Avebury's monument dates from about 1800 years B.C. The stones are sarsen, the hard sandstone still found lying about in the locality as slabs or boulders. Although the stones themselves are not nearly so large as those of Stonehenge, the complex itself is far larger. Unfortunately, many of the stones have been disturbed, laid flat, buried, or simply removed, probably because the Christians of the Middle Ages viewed them as part of pagan rituals. The site has long been known and valued by antiquarians, however, and it is known that King Charles II was persuaded to visit.

Cows at Avebury

The small museum there was presided over by

an elderly man, assisted, we were glad to note, by a young enthusiast whose parents were inhabitants of the village. "They live just outside the ring," the older man said with approval, "so they are not crazy, like all the folk who live within it." The youngster grinned patiently. I noticed after we had left that the tickets we had been issued for admission to the museum were of different colors, and that mine was a child's ticket.

Our next stop was a castle of considerably more modern origin, High Clere, the Victorian mansion belonging to the family of the Fifth Earl of Carnarvon, who discovered King Tut's tomb. The Earl was buried

Avebury

on Beacon Hill, site of an Iron Age hill fort. He died far away at the site of his famous excavation from an infected mosquito bite, and his early demise gave rise to the belief that he Tomb was cursed.

The grounds were widespread and the home itself huge, situated at the end of its own road, which was probably two miles long. Several workers were readying for a fête to be held the following day, and the home itself was closed. The wind was cold, and the rain, though slackened since we had stopped at an inn for a very hearty lunch, was still misting. The meal, our first of the trip, was delicious and ample. This was a good surprise, since our earlier trips had not supplied us with much delectable food. It had been healthful enough, I suppose, but the vegetables offered at this time of year had been limited to "spring greens," a tasteless mélange of whatever had been growing on the grounds, cooked too long. We had no reservations for the night, so we drove on to Bradford-on-Avon, where Mark had several times visited his friend Roger. Roger, however, was in Spain, and it was about five when we arrived, so we did not attempt to call his wife. Instead we found the Riverside Inn, situated on the fabled waterway, and collapsed into bed, where we slept long and soundly, although our host had been concerned that the live band performing beneath us would be disturbing. After our extremely early commencement of the day, I doubt anything short of an earthquake would have kept us awake.

Next morning it was still raining, so although the city's inhabitants were walking along the path by the river just outside our window and our hosts recommended the historic sites we would find if we followed their lead, we drove on after breakfast. Our destination was the Friends School at Sidcot, where our friends Sally and Jim had spent the previous year, Sally as the school nurse, and Jim underemployed as a sort of maintenance man, while their two daughters were students.

    Sally had asked us to deliver some gifts to her friend Grace, a retired teacher from the school. We had visualized a small school, probably housed in a picturesque cottage built of native stone, and were therefore stunned when the building, surrounded by scaffolding, was of a size sufficient to accommodate several hundred students, one of whom was deputized to lead us to the Head's office, who, we were told, could tell us how to find Grace's cottage. The trip to his office was long and roundabout, leading through a couple of buildings, and the student apologized for the delay, explaining that he had never been to the office himself.

    He persevered and found the place, and Angus, the young Scotsman who was the quite new headmaster, greeted us warmly and called Grace, who came promptly to fetch us. She was, as Sally and Jim had foretold, gracious and delightful. She called a friend, Ethel, whose husband had taught at the school until his recent death, and both joined us for lunch at a restaurant nearby. Grace had an air of unshakeable serenity, in spite of having nursed an ailing husband for fourteen years while teaching full time. Ethel, who invited us to her home for a post-luncheon cup of tea, showed us the sculptures created by her late husband, who had been both a pilot and teacher. Both women were looking forward to a trip to the States in October, and we issued a most sincere invitation for them to visit us.

We drove on toward Taunton and the dairy farm/bed and breakfast where we had spent a week about fourteen years before. We planned to be at the train station in time to pick up our friends Randi and Bjorn Heggsett. When we arrived at the farm, however, they were already there to greet us, their train having taken less time than they had expected. Chris, the dairyman/host, had put aside his constant cow work to retrieve them. It was a wonderful reunion, and Randi and Bjorn were remarkably unchanged after a sixteen-year span since we had met them in Norway and spent one afternoon and evening with them in Lom, the village where we had spent National Day.

It had been quite a few years since we had seen them, and their son Erlend, whom we remembered as an apple-cheeked two year-old, had grown to be eighteen and was enduring his year in the Norwegian armed service. There was additional news, for he had decided that if, as a vegetarian, he could not bear to think of an animal's life being sacrificed, he surely could not bring himself to take a human life in the unlikely event Norway ever asked him to do so. He had therefore only the week before asked for and received release from the armed forces and assignment to alternate service as a conscientious objector. We had never met his fourteen-year-old brother Erik, but hoped someday we would.

Now they joined us for a stroll up the country lane where the hedgerows were spilling over with Bluebells, Campion, Queen Anne's Lace, and Lords-and-Ladies. Apple trees were flowering, the black-and-white cows were lowing, and all was very much as I recalled it. But one activity was gone. The eggs I had sought in the garden and the hedges were not here this year, for the foxes had eaten all the hens.

The following day we had lunch with Katrina Thompson, who had been a wonderful friend to our grandson Edward. She was as described. Her husband, however, was hardly the slender, ascetic vicar I had envisioned. Instead he was a hearty, retired Army man, a raconteur who seemed to enjoy our company in spite of the pain he was suffering after a fall four days before. His hip had been operated on twice unsuccessfully, and then a third attempt had worked, but during a church service he had tripped over a rug and injured the hip again. The doctor was hopeful, however, that further surgery would not be necessary.

Katrina showed us about their grounds, a lovely wooded area where wild flowers abounded, including Cowslips, small yellow flowers often mentioned in literature but now, she told us, quite rare. Lemon-yellow primroses, which we had been too late to find during our earlier trips, were abundant now, as were white-flowering Haw. There was even a distant glimpse of the sea.

After lunch we drove to the coast at Portland. By now the weather was clear and sunny, and the water was the azure of the Caribbean. We followed the coastline and stopped to introduce Bjorn and Randi to the Swannery, where monks about five centuries ago had established a large Benedictine monastery. The monastery was long gone, with many of the stones now to be found in the houses in the nearby village of Abbotsbury. The Swannery remained, with currently 137 nesting pairs of the huge, graceful white birds –

their eggs were about five times the size of a hen's egg. The colony flourished on the swamp at the end of the Fleet. Eel grass and other vegetation which appealed to them grew here, and the human visitors did not seem to disturb the females, who were sometimes aided in the construction of their haphazard brush piles by the attendants. Although visitors were warned that the birds are fiercely territorial, they seemed to realize that the staff had their interests at heart. We watched one of the men roust a mother from her nest because one of her seven eggs had rolled out of brooding distance. He expertly shoved the egg back into place. The swans' only enemies were minks – visitors are asked to alert the staff if they saw these predators anywhere about.

Parents pushing a twin baby carriage next attracted my attention, for we were expecting twin great-grandsons to be born while we were away. These English babies were girls, thirteen weeks old, very small and swaddled for protection against the chill wind. They smiled, and their parents said they themselves were just beginning to recover. They had had a live-in maternity nurse for ten weeks, without whom, they reported, life would have been sleepless and generally impossible.

Next morning we renewed acquaintance with another spot we had discovered and loved on an earlier trip – Cothelstone Hill. It was still overcast and windy, but the view from the top provided a wonderful view of Taunton Deane, with green fields stretching out for miles, punctuated with brilliant yellow squares, the false sunlight of rape pastures. We were lucky to come when these were covered with yellow flowers.

A group of six small and sturdy ponies wandered near the summit, completely unconcerned by our presence. We passed the entrance to Cothelstone Manor, where, in stark and bloody contrast to the present serenity of the place, two of the followers of the Duke of Monmouth had been hanged after their defeat at the Battle of Sedgemoor in 1686. Although the infamous Judge Jeffreys had been aware that one of the victims had taken no part in the Battle, he said that the family owed the victors a body. They got it.

We said goodbye to Bjorn and Randi, with urgent invitations to visit us in the spring, and went to visit Jefferson and Frani Horsley, whose brother Alexander was our friend in Atlanta. They had hosted a memorable dinner for us on our previous visit, and we were eager to have them to lunch. They had moved a few doors from the home we had seen before, and while Jefferson was an officeholder in Taunton and was totally occupied with an upcoming election, Frani devoted her energies to a garden with tall, sturdy borders of Lunaria, showers of Spiraea, pale pink Clematis, bluebells and Weigelia. Inside in the sun room, she sheltered an amazing collection of tropical plants, including Hibiscus, Oleander, and Bougainvillia, and others hopefully brought home from Italy and Spain. They thrived there but did not bloom. However, Geraniums, Christmas Cactus and Poinsettia did.

Then we returned to our dairy farm, where Holsteins contentedly wandered the meadow behind the house. Much had changed since our earlier visit. The house had been enlarged to encompass the shed and the hayloft, but the view we fondly recalled across the road still had the same flowering apple trees, beneath which sheep grazed. Jim, the son whom we remembered as a chubby ten-year-old, was now a strong young man in his mid-twenties, so reliable a helper at the farm that his parents, Chris and Maureen, were anticipating a holiday in Australia in the fall.

The following morning we drove to Lydford Gorge, a National Trust property. The small, somnolent nearby village of Lydford had once been the site of a large tin mine. A large castle had been built to serve as a prison for workers who disobeyed company rules. No trace of it remained, not too surprising since it was built in 1102. After the tin was depleted, the gorge left behind became feared as the home of a family named Gubbins, fearsome outlaws known for their "lewdness." Still later it became known as a place of pilgrimage. Now it provided a well-kept but challenging walk through moss-covered grounds to a ninety-foot waterfall known as the White Lady. Many of the usual wildflowers bordered the path, including brilliant white clusters of blossoms which resembled Bluebells but which I later identified as Wild Garlic.

We joined the National Trust here, urged by a very eager salesman, and during the rest of our trip found it to be a sound investment, for it provided free parking and a free ticket to many of the places we visited.

Driving through Dartmoor, we passed pastures of sparse grass and gorse, where often cows, sheep and horses grazed together while buzzards soared beneath constantly changing gray clouds. And our route toward the Sidcot School took us to a most spectacular sight. A small sign mentioned quietly that Cheddar Gorge lay ahead. The solitary road we travelled led through country where the only inhabitants seemed to be an occasional fox or a pheasant crossing the road. Our way descended steadily, and the chalk cliffs on either side grew steeper until they towered 450 feet above us. The Gorge had been formed thousands of years ago by a river which was now hidden underground. As we emerged from the Gorge, we found the village of Cheddar nestled at the far end.

  We paused at Dartmeet, where two branches of the Dart River came together. The remains of an ancient bridge, roughly fashioned of stones embedded in the river, were left next to a newer bridge. Brightly colored Chaffinches lit very near, and a friendly Brit pointed out that the color of the water, similar to long-brewed tea, was the result of peat. Penstemon and a pale pink bell-shaped flower called Lady's Frock flourished here.

  Grace and Ethel, one recently retired as a teacher and the other the widow of a teacher at Sidcot School, greeted us most graciously as we arrived to deliver some gifts from Jim and Sally, who had spent the previous year at the school. Grace gave us tea before we went to meet her friend Ethel at a restaurant for lunch. After that we were invited to Ethel's for more tea and admired their beloved and meticulously tended gardens. We made plans to welcome them to Georgia in the autumn.

 Our way next led us across the Tamar River, a broad waterway which for centuries separated Cornwall from the rest of Britain. The southernmost land in England, Cornwall is semi-tropical in selected places, although the wind, constantly blowing from the water, is fierce, and its rocky shores have been the sites of hundreds of shipwrecks. Our destination was Coombe Farm near Looe, misnamed but very lovely. There were peacocks strutting about the grounds, a flock of white doves and four dogs, but nary a farm animal. Larger than our other bed and breakfast houses, this one accommodated twenty guests, and we discovered, as before, that the English will never speak first, but almost always are friendly and informative conversationalists once spoken to. One quite elderly lady insisted that she could teach us to read her native Welsh within minutes, but her daughter, a writer of historical novels, shook her head firmly, and we did not take advantage of her offer. A very attractive young German couple had somehow found their way there, and although we tried hard to find out more about one another, their English and my German were about equal, in other words, pathetic.

The following morning provided renewed acquaintance with the incredibly narrow tracks which serve as roads in Cornwall. These thoroughfares were sufficiently wide to fit a couple of donkey carts, and in a pinch two subcompact cars, but meeting a large farm vehicle necessitates backing up, sometimes as much as a quarter of a mile. No one ever, so far as we could see, expressed any impatience with this procedure, and a hand salute seemed to qualify as thanks to the backer-upper.

The hedgerows completely enclosing the roads were ten feet high at least, covered with Pink Campion, Bluebells, Daisies, Lords-and-Ladies, and Haw. It was like driving through a constant garden.

Ancient bridge

We were learning the hard way not to follow slavishly all directions to National Trust Sites, many of which were impossible to find. We did manage to find Point Pill, a rather unimpressive waterway, which by the time we finally got there was low and muddy, with the tide at its ebb.

Some things had changed in the fifteen years since we were last here, so that Fowey, which we recalled as a tiny village, was now a thriving tourist metropolis, which we fled after the ferry crossing. We made our way to a National Trust Car Park, which could handle about twenty vehicles, at Pencarrow Point. From there we wandered down a soggy path to join the Coast Path atop the cliffs overlooking the sea.

Gulls wheeled overhead, and the water was a brilliant blue. We did not see another soul, and only a distant church steeple gave evidence that any other humans had ever frequented the area. This Coast Path, which was not oppressively well-tended and is sometimes difficult to discern, ran for miles.

Our next stop was at The Aviary, near Redruth. This would hardly seem to qualify as a Hotel, though it was thus listed in our Bed and Breakfast Guide. There were only six guest rooms available, and we found at dinner that two of them were occupied by a girl who worked for a pharmaceutical firm and a young man who was there on business. He worked for the British Broadcasting Company, and although he began by being quite silent, he turned out to be quite informative.

When we spoke of the very noisy gravel across which Dalgleish and other detectives of British television mysteries walked and which often obscured their conversation, he told us that there were actually four different gravel paths, each only about ten feet long and housed in the BBC studio, and each containing different sizes of gravel. There are also, he told us, four or five doors, leading nowhere but providing the proper sound when shut. One is carefully equipped with a squeak.

The other guest, an idealistic girl, was young

enough to be frantic at the lack of research conducted by the pharmaceutical firm for which she worked. She was also disturbed by its enormous profits.

The following morning was crystal clear, and the sun shone brightly on the well-tended and colorful gardens surrounding the Aviary. We walked down a public footpath which separated the grounds of our lodging from pastures where cows were munching very green grass. We encountered only one member of the public as we strolled, a very old and lame gentleman out for his morning constitutional. He remarked on the weather with wonder and appreciation.

Several natives spoke of the upcoming eclipse scheduled for August. It would be the first total eclipse since 1927, and it was estimated that one million visitors would come to admire it. Most of our informants themselves intended to flee the neighborhood.

We stopped at the Bedruthian Steps, rocks which resembled the stairway of a huge giant, which is who Bedruthian was. The sea crashed below the cliff where we stood, and the sparse grass had many low-growing flowers, battered by the wind but persisting.

The sea is always near in Cornwall, and a newly ploughed field was completely white with gulls gathered to enjoy the worms who had been brought to the surface. We walked to Pentire Farms, a National Trust holding, where a sign informed us that grazing sheep, who seemed undisturbed by our presence, could literally be frightened to death by a strange dog. As we drove along the usual country lanes, with the usual flowers in the hedgerows, we noted a new addition to the floral arrangement, a brilliant blue blossom later identified as Borage. It was also startling, as we drove toward Delabole, to come upon ten windmills, all making use of the constant commodity hereabouts. We stopped and read a sign by a small, unoccupied building reading, "Windpower is a clean technology. Green electricity. Construction to begin on a purpose-built renewable energy centre, to be opened in late summer 2000." This was both hopeful and surprising, for we had had the feeling, driving day after day through the unhurried and unchanging countryside, that modernity was centuries in the future. Still, we thought it was what was not here that made the place so lovely. There was not a telephone pole nor a single billboard. I wondered if it was possible to drive in the States for any distance without encountering either of these.

    The signs directing us to National Trust sites were small and very few, but we managed to find our way to High Cliff, above the west coast of Cornwall. That evening we stopped at an over-named "hotel," actually a house situated on a small lot, from which we learned how much could be grown on a few square feet. Not only was there a beautiful garden, but also sixteen hens, several kittens, and a horse!

    We drove on to Taunton Beach. The chilly early morning found us fairly well bundled up, but the weather did not deter some hardy (or insane) British surfers. I found some interestingly patterned snail shells on the dry sand, quite far from the water, and tucked them in my pocket. As we were leaving, I noticed a sign at the Braunton Burrows Conservation Area forbidding "Naturist Activities." I assumed in my innocence that I should jolly well have left the snail shells where I found them, and indeed I should have, because later I discovered that they were inhabited by smelly snails. We later found that the forbidden "naturist activities" meant nudity. We hunkered, fully clothed, behind a sand dune for Britt to change film, and even so the breeze blew sand into the camera.

We had lunch at Lynmouth, a resort where hundreds of Brits, most of them elderly and lame, were doggedly ignoring the weather, which by that time had degenerated into a heavy rain. We stopped at an antique inn for sandwiches and were seated at a table next to a couple of about our age, a wife who smiled silently as her garrulous husband immediately embarked on a lengthy tale about his great-grandfather, who had travelled from England in 1863 to Salt Lake City with his fourteen year old daughter to join the Mormons (a word which he pronounced with the accent on the second syllable). When Brigham Young wished to add the daughter to his collection of wives, however, they had returned to England and the Anglican Church.

That evening we lucked upon a wonderful Bed and Breakfast at Berrow Links, near Burnham. No one was home, but the surroundings were so attractive that we decided to wait until a Friedland, as we thought from the name plate on the door, came home. We were rewarded quite shortly when a very tall, very blonde and beautiful girl drove in. She was bewildered when we asked if she were Miss Friedland – it turned out that her name was something else altogether, and the nameplate identified the maker of the lock.

She welcomed us in anyway and showed us a luxurious room, and later we met her mother, an ardent golfer who had been playing on the course across the road. There was a unique objet d'art on the table where we breakfasted, a golf ball glued to a small plate. It was, our hostess told us, the ball with which she had shot a hole in one, and a very expensive one, for it had been shot at a tournament with eighty-five participants – she explained that it was customary for anyone who achieved an ace to treat all the other players to drinks.

Our route the next day led us to Wales and Wenalli Farm by way of the Wye River Valley, where we saw the site of Winthour's impossible leap. This feat occurred during the Civil War in 1642. Winthour, a royalist, was being pursued by Cromwell's men. He and his horse jumped several hundred feet into the Wye River, swam across and made it to safety in Wales on the other side.

After some confusion with the routes, we finally arrived at the Forest of Deane, which was a bit of a disappointment – just a few fairly young trees. I suppose one can understand the Brits' excessive appreciation of almost any tree when one realizes that this once heavily forested nation now has only 8% of its land left forested, half now owned by the State. Later, in looking over information about the vicinity acquired at the pub where we lunched, we found that there was a Hodnet Estate and Gardens nearby which we would have wanted to see for ancestral reasons. Too late, for we had already reached our lodgings, near Abergevenny in Wales. The main house was built in 1565 and had a huge stone fireplace, where after dinner we enjoyed an unexpected meeting of minds.

Our first meeting with our fellow guests was

probably equally unpromising on both sides. He was an extremely tattooed fellow with a ponytail and a virtually incompre-hensible Cockney accent. She was a beautiful black girl with lovely long legs displayed to advantage in the shortest skirt I'd ever seen. Lord knows what they expected of us, an elderly pair of Americans with southern accents!

We both got a lesson against leaping to conclusions when we discovered in conversation at dinner that we read the same books, shared the same opinions on foreign policy, and were generally soul mates. We talked in front of that fireplace until far into the night.

The bird feeder outside the window at breakfast attracted sparrows similar to ours back home, and Blue Tits and the by-now-familiar Chaffinches. We drove on the next day through the Brecon Beacons in the Taf Fawr Valley, where sheep were grazing on what appeared to be very sparse pickings.

Then we went in search of Skomer Island, where we hoped to take a boat ride and find Puffins. Our information did not tell us that this is an all-day excursion, for which we arrived far too late. We remembered an earlier search for Puffins some years before on an island off the Gaspé Peninsula that had proved equally fruitless, for that day the wind had been too high and the boat had stayed at dock. We had finally found the adorable clownlike birds in a fjord in Alaska.

However, we drove along a spectacular coast to St. David's Head, where we were told that literally hundreds of seals gathered near a lighthouse, and saw swimmers defying hypothermia. Next morning at

Mother & child

breakfast at Ynes (pronounced Ennis) Barry Hotel, a family told us that they had been among the swimmers and had, by the time we met them fourteen hours later, almost thawed out. At our dinner the night before at our hotel, we ate our first traditional fish and chips, and they were great. We were also treated to a dessert called "No Hanky–Panky," a sinfully tasty chocolate concoction.

     Next day we were successful in finding Carreg Samson. This small prehistoric rock structure, an outstanding Neolithic burial chamber 3000 years old, sat on three of its original seven uprights. The legend goes that Samson lifted the capstone, sixteen feet long, into place with his little finger. It was now surrounded with cows. We did not know that this was a Bank Holiday weekend, and it led to near-disaster, for we could not find lodgings anywhere near the resort country. Having been turned away from three very isolated Beds and Breakfasts, the last of which was just putting up its No Vacancy sign when we approached, we were just resigning ourselves to spending the night in our tiny automobile when we saw a sign promising a bed and followed a crazily circuitous route to Enys Barry, bless its heart.

    Travelling in the U.K. had other difficulties. Several bed-and-breakfasts who had promised to honor credit cards had abandoned the practice by the time we got there because of excessive administrative costs. When hosts agreed to take travellers cheques, figuring out the exchange rate proved to be a mathematical mess, with the rate changing daily. It was also a challenge following picturesque routes using inadequate maps. After considerable teeth gnashing, brilliant Britt always proved his capability in both areas. Also, English folks were so helpful, not only in giving route directions but also in offering additional services such as bringing our car keys into a pub when we had left them in the car!

    I tried to decipher signs in Welsh, which bears no relation to any language I ever saw. Examples are milltir = miles, tooledau = toilet, canol y def = town centre, diwedd = end, Plwmp = town name.

    At Furnace, which we greeted joyfully as the only destination we had been able to pronounce in a while, we admired and took pictures of a lovely waterfall, which had powered the bellows which heated the furnace which melted iron in the 1750 mill alongside. After fifty years, the iron melting had been abandoned and the mill turned to agricultural purposes.

At our next stop, in Llanegryn, it was startling to find that our host, a gentle man named David Sylvester, was a clone of our son John. The weather was sunny and warm, and the bright yellow of the Gorse contrasted with the gray stone used in all construction. The Sylvesters, like all of our hosts in Wales, were transplants from England. Mrs. Sylvester told us that many of the original, very old inhabitants of the tiny village had never left its boundaries during their long lives. We walked from the house on a path which led to a wonderful clump of Bluebells by a stream and then climbed a steep slope to an ancient church. Our fellow guests were two couples from Yorkshire, all teachers who came to the district to climb. We found that the Bed and Breakfast at Bourton-on-the-Water where we had a reservation was the same one at which they had stayed the year before. The room where one couple had slept contained the four-poster bed of which we had read in the description in our book. They said we might well be inundated by the multitude of stuffed animals piled upon the bed, and they had been amused and horrified by the picture of Minnie Mouse hung above it.

Sure enough, we met Minnie that night and discovered that our hostess had travelled to North Carolina to take a class in doll making and had created all the dolls and creatures herself. She probably thought travelling overseas to find Bluebells was equally silly! She told us that when lost in the wilds of North Carolina she had asked directions of a native, demanding to know the best route to Cheyenne, when she had meant to

Nan among the bluebells

say Cherokee. He guessed, in the best English fashion, that she was "not from around here."

The water which flowed through Bourton was the Windrush River, which was home to numerous Mallard ducks, proudly leading their young, and often, our hostess told us, causing traffic jams as they sauntered across the roads. A Chaffinch challenged its image in the mirror of a car.

The next day we stayed in the Cotswolds, driving to Cerney Gardens, a place completely unmarked, but we drove up a private drive which we figured had to be it. The drive led to a large home, and as we parked there, wondering where to go next, a pleasant, middle-aged woman, dressed comfortably in a stained sweatshirt, jeans, and well-worn tennis shoes, came out to greet us. She turned out to be

Lady Angus, and after she had chatted a bit, she guided us to her daughter's house, where she said someone would offer us coffee. She had always lived in the neighborhood, but told us they had only purchased the house three years ago. It had been built with mill money. She introduced us to her "Cotswold Sheep," a variety hardly ever seen nowadays. They were quite large, and she explained that the joints they produced were more suitable to large Victorian families than today's nuclear ones. We had the impression that she was lonely, for she talked quite a while, apologizing for the morning's chilly weather and recounting that it had been so wonderfully sunny the day before that the family had been able to gather on the terrace to celebrate Lord Angus's birthday.

    Her son Simon then arrived, tugged by a very large and rambunctious Newfoundland who leaped upon me and then dragged him on toward the garden. We followed another drive and found our way to the display gardens. There was no one in sight to accept our fee, which we dropped in a box labelled for the purpose, and we wandered for an hour or so admiring the flowers, many new to us, and took pictures of a yellow Tree Peony and some glorious blue Anemones, as well as a stone ruin covered with pale pink Clematis.

    We stopped for lunch at an inn, and our waitress spoke nostalgically of time spent in Telluride in Colorado. We were surprised at how many of the folks we met had visited the States and seemed eager to return.

    Next we visited a Roman villa near Chedworth. The portions excavated of this fourth century home were very well-preserved, although it had been buried for centuries before its discovery early in the nineteen hundreds. An elegant farm had once been there, inhabited not by the Romans, but by British farmers who had emulated the lifestyle of their conquerors, imported mosaic tiles from Chichester, and devoted much time to bathing. There were elaborate systems for heating the water. Since the Romans occupied Britain for more than four centuries, beginning 35 years before Christ, it was not too amazing that more than fifty such villas had been unearthed. Excavation was continuing.

    We travelled on to Suddeley Castle gardens. The castle itself was now in ruins, but the gardens had been restored. Although the castle was never owned by royalty, it was often visited by them. One garden was called the Queens', because three queens had once walked there: first Catherine Parr, sixth and last wife of Henry VIII, then his daughter Elizabeth I, and the young nine-days' queen, Lady Jane Grey.

    There was a distinct Persian influence on the garden designs, brought home by the Crusaders. Cromwell, curse his wretched memory, destroyed many gardens throughout England, for he felt they made political statements of which he disapproved. The designs were preserved, however, and with the Restoration of the Stuarts, many were replanted.

    Our last stop was a reunion visit to Hidcote Gardens, near Chipping Campden. Our first sight of these incredible gardens had been fifteen years earlier, and then Britt deserved a medal for managing to shove me and a wheelchair and a broken ankle through the many "rooms" which comprised the ten acres. Now it was simpler and even lovelier than we recalled.

The garden was laid out over seventy years ago by a retired American military officer, Major Lawrence Johnson. We had two brochures, both of which told us that the gardens opened at ten in the morning, but when we arrived promptly, we found the place locked up tight. One of the staff informed us casually that the hour had been changed to eleven. She seemed rather unconcerned, and, indeed, the pace of rural England is serenely slow, so that an hour one way or the other does not matter. To them. She suggested that we walk through the adjoining village while we waited, so we did, and admired some white ducks who spread their wings in an odd fashion, obviously to impress females. Then we wandered further to a farm where an elderly man was engaged in the seemingly endless task of weeding an immense strawberry bed. When we finally were allowed into the garden we stopped to chat with a gardener. It was amazing that a team of seven, temporarily reduced to six, could manage to keep the place in such order.

Our last overnight lodging had been chosen for its proximity to Gatwick Airport, only half an hour drive away. Bulmer Farm was deep in the country, at Holmbury St. Mary, Surrey, and our host, David Hill, was a charming and thoughtful gentleman. His wife, however, was indescribably rude. We had a taste of life in the village when we were told that there had been a funeral that afternoon for a woman, Nancy Collinson, who had died at ninety-three, having worked as a housekeeper for a nearby family until the last day.

There were two floral arrangements, brought

from the church after the service, in the kitchen sink when we arrived, and David explained that the formal one had been done by their florist daughter-in-law, and the smaller collection of roadside wild flowers, in a tumbler, was the work of two granddaughters, aged four and six, who had been great friends of the old lady.

    We had dinner at an inn close by and were finishing our desserts when four muscular young men came in. The bartender greeted them warmly, and they ordered "the usual" to be served at nine, and then hurried out. The bartender explained that they worked in London, drove their bicycles down after work, then rode them for nine miles or so through the woodland paths before dinner.

    The next day, alas, we got on a plane and bid farewell again, this time for good, to my land of dreams. It was time to go home.

Afterword

The British Isles will always hold a special place in my heart. But my trips to the United Kingdom have also given me a renewed perception and appreciation of my native Georgia. I have several times stood on the shore of a barrier island and looked over the Atlantic, remembering. I have watched playful dolphins, looked for a right whale, and enjoyed the fruitfulness of a salt marsh. Other times, Britt and I have ventured to the mountains of north Georgia, which are as ancient, after all, as any in England, Scotland or Wales. Today I mostly tend my garden on my hilltop home in Atlanta, and there is a world of enjoyment there, too. Somehow, my discovery of the British Isles has led to a renewed perception and appreciation of the entire world.

www.ingramcontent.com/pod-product-compliance
Lightning Source LLC
Chambersburg PA
CBHW051838090426
42736CB00011B/1859